The S.... Learner

The Slow Learner

SOME EDUCATIONAL
PRINCIPLES AND POLICIES

BY

M. F. Cleugh

*Reader in the Teaching
of Educationally Subnormal Children,
University of London, Institute of Education*

METHUEN & CO. LTD
11 NEW FETTER LANE, LONDON E.C.4

First published in 1957
Second edition with corrections published in 1968
2.1
SBN 416 04150 7

First published as an Educational Paperback in 1968
1.1
SBN 416 04160 4

Printed in Great Britain by
Butler & Tanner Ltd
Frome and London

Author's Note

I should like to thank those many people who have, wittingly or unwittingly, helped to evolve the point of view set out in this book. My major debt is to Mrs S. M. Gray, Miss K. L. Hanks, and Miss F. A. Lloyd, but there are others too numerous to mention who in discussion groups and private conversations have contributed suggestions, criticisms, and challenging disagreements.

M.C.

Whittington, Salop
October 1956

IN MEMORY OF
MY PARENTS

Contents

PART I: SPECIAL SCHOOLS

page

I Introduction   1

II Ascertainment   6

III The Organisation of Classes in E.S.N. Schools   30

IV Reorganisation in E.S.N. Schools   40

V De-ascertainment   51

VI Seriously Handicapped Children   67

PART II: ORDINARY SCHOOLS

VII The Setting and Scope of the Problem in Ordinary Schools   84

VIII 'Ordinary' Educational Treatment   95

IX Methods of Providing Special Educational Treatment in Ordinary Schools   115

X Remedial Measures   140

XI A Note on the Training of Teachers   160

Selected References   183

Index   185

Preface

When a book such as this is reprinted, decisions about terminology have to be made. The Ministry of Education is now the Department of Education and Science, children formerly called ineducable are now 'unsuitable for education at school'—these are just two examples of the numerous, small verbal changes that would be needed to make this book sound as if it was written in 1967. But it *wasn't* written in 1967, and it seemed more important to retain its internal consistency at the possible cost of sounding outdated than to tinker endlessly with the terminology. The same holds for statistics—to replace those given for example on page 9 by more recent ones would probably end by being more confusing than helpful to the reader. (It is interesting to note that in spite of the many new E.S.N. schools that have been built since 1955 little impression has been made on the waiting list—which tends to suggest that the remarks made in the text about the very wide definition of 'E.S.N.' have been justified by events.)

An exception to this general policy must, however, be made with the important changes introduced by the Mental Health Act of 1959. The latter part of Chapter 5 and the whole of Chapter 6 have been rewritten to incorporate changes made by the Act.

CHAPTER I

Introduction

THE first provision in England for mentally handicapped children came with the opening of the Royal Earlswood Institution in 1848, but it was not until 1892 that the first day school for educable mental deficients was started by the School Board of Leicester. In the years that have elapsed since then there have been many changes, both in the provisions for deviant children and in the educational philosophy that underlies those provisions. In an age when all children were expected to conform to set standards only the most marked deviants could hope to escape the general lock-step, and it is not surprising that the early special schools were thought of as abnormal places attended by grossly abnormal children, nor that they were often regarded as dumping grounds to relieve the ordinary school, rather than as educational establishments in their own right. Traces of both these attitudes still remain today, but, one hopes, in a less blatant form. Nowadays in theory (if not always in practice) an attempt is made to distinguish between educable slow learners and the low-grade ineducables, and to exclude the latter: to separate out those whose school failure is primarily due to physical handicap or emotional difficulty or misbehaviour or absence, from the genuine slow learners and to make separate provision for them; and to evolve an educational philosophy which starts from the needs of each deviant child rather than from a lock-step system which rejects him.

Over a period of years, the evolution has been considerable, and it is a natural evolution. It stands to reason that in any field, the most glaring handicaps are the ones which first cry out for attention and when these have been dealt with lesser degrees of deviation can then be noticed and attended to: thus the blind are noticed before the partially-sighted and the totally deaf and badly crippled before those whose handicaps are slighter. Similarly, 'mental deficiency' is replaced by the broader concept of 'educational subnormality', and the untenable notion that a very small proportion are abnormal while all the rest are utterly and entirely similar and suited to an academic curriculum is replaced by the notion of a graduated continuum in which a large minority may need special educational treatment. Much of this change is due to psychological discoveries: some of it to a greater liberalism of educational thought, as for instance in the 'child-centred school' movement; and some of it simply to the lessons of experience of universal education. When schooling is compulsory for all children, the full range of individual variation is brought inescapably to the notice of the Authorities, in a way which is not possible when exceptions are allowed, as it is just the bottom 10 per cent which is most likely to be seriously underrepresented in such circumstances. Three-quarters of a century's experience of the working of the Education Act of 1870 showed clearly the need for making more allowance for individual differences, and led to the Education Act of 1944 with its stress on the 'three A's'. Here we are not concerned with the implications of the 1944 Act as regards brighter children, but with the wide diversity of provision which it encourages and enjoins for the slow and the dull.

Each Local Authority must make special educational treatment available for all children who need it. The categories of such handicapped children are defined in Regulations and revised from time to time, and among these categories the one we are concerned with is: 'Educationally Subnormal Pupils, that is to say, pupils who by reason of limited ability or other conditions resulting in educational retardation, require some specialised form of education wholly or partly in substitution for the education normally given in ordinary schools.' This specialised form of education may be given in special E.S.N. schools recognised by the Minister or arrangements may be made to give children special educational treatment within ordinary schools. In the latter case, the Regulations state that the special treatment provided for every handicapped pupil shall be appropriate to his disability. The Ministry's Pamphlet on *Special Educational Treatment* adds, 'In the past, arrangements for dealing with dull and backward children have been made on the assumption that there were few of these, and that something makeshift might serve their purpose. It is now realised that they are many, probably as many as are suitable for grammar school education, and something at once more permanent and more carefully considered is needed.'[1]

The 1944 Act has therefore naturally resulted in a great expansion of the special services for backward children. New special schools have been built and old ones enlarged: development plans have included schemes for special educational treatment in ordinary schools; experimental remedial centres have been set up: Local Education Authorities and other bodies have organised many courses for teachers on backwardness and allied problems: and publishers have produced books which it is claimed are particularly suitable for backward children. In all this welter of activity, it is inevitable that there should be some confusion and some false starts, promising trails that lead nowhere, premature claims for this or that method or organisation; and it seemed worth while at this point to examine the various ways of providing special educational treatment in order to determine the merits and disadvantages of each type of organisation.

It is quite evident that a book of this kind, dealing only

[1] Pamphlet No. 5, p. 23.

with policies, and not with personalities or methods, is leaving out much that is most important in education. What really matters is what goes on in the school or class and the relationships it engenders, not how it is organised or how the children who attend it are selected. This is true in any education and it is doubly true in special education, where the informing spirit is more than ever vital and 'the letter killeth'.

Nevertheless even though organisation is only a framework in which the vital activities are carried on, there is a case for making it as suitable and efficient a framework as possible. A good teacher will do good work even in a bad system, and a poor teacher will render ineffective the opportunities provided by even the most suitable organisation, but granting all this, it still remains true that he can be helped or hindered by the conditions in which he has to work and it is only common sense that these should be made as helpful as possible. An instructive example is provided by Miss Taylor's book *Experiments with a Backward Class*. From her description, there is no doubt that sound work was done in gaining the interest and co-operation of the children, and this is the main thing. Yet the organisation left much to be desired. The heterogeneous collection of children, and the absence of selection policy other than nuisance value, while it accurately mirrors conditions that still too often obtain, made the teacher's task unnecessarily difficult. It would be unfortunate if the success of her book led others to assume that the organisation, as well as the methods, should be uncritically copied.

In this book, I have deliberately limited myself to discussing principles of policy and organisation, while fully realising that these are part only, and the less important part at that, of providing any special educational treatment that is really worth the name. Yet within its limited field I hope that it may fulfil a useful function. It may be objected that, since each deviant child has unique needs, generalisations are unprofitable. But

4

to establish any school, special or otherwise, Authorities must have some idea of the sort of children for whom it is intended, i.e. they must have policy and principles to guide them. Their policy need not be rigid, but neither should it be hand-to-mouth. The children are all exceptional in one way or another, and in a literal sense it will be 'the exceptions that prove the rule', and establish the wisdom or otherwise of the provisions that are made: yet this does not mean that no general statements are admissible. I have tried to show that certain policies or types of school organisation are often helpful, but this does not mean that they are to be advocated in all circumstances, and it seems to me a useful task to discuss principles of organisation for slow learners even though (or particularly because) they are not rules to be followed blindly.

I propose to discuss, first, the problems that attend the transfer of children to a special school, ascertainment, the organisation of classes in special schools, and the decision that arises at school leaving age between the alternatives of de-ascertainment and reporting to the Mental Health Committee. Later, the various forms that the provision of special educational treatment may take in ordinary schools will be considered in turn, together with adjuncts such as remedial centres. Finally, some aspects of the training of teachers are discussed.

At the outset, I must make it clear that the comments, criticisms, and suggestions are in no way official, nor do they necessarily reflect the policy of those Authorities from whose practices I have learned most. They are simply the opinions of a private individual whose work takes her into a number of schools embodying different types of special provision for slow learners, and who has had unusually good opportunities for detailed and free discussion with teachers from different areas and learned from their experience as well as from her own, where the shoe is most likely to pinch in different types of organisation.

CHAPTER II

Ascertainment

U NDER Section 34 of the Education Act of 1944 it is laid down as a duty of Local Education Authorities to ascertain what children in their area require special educational treatment (not merely those who may need to attend a special school). Having discovered the full extent of the need, the Authority is then in a position to make suitable provision for all these children, and to decide which ones can most profitably occupy special school places and which ones can be adequately catered for by other arrangements, e.g. in ordinary schools.

An educationally subnormal child, it is suggested in the Ministry's Pamphlet No. 5, is one whose *attainments* are less than 80 per cent of the normal for his age: this includes all dull children whose I.Q.'s are less than 80, and also any other children of *whatever grade of intelligence* whose attainments are seriously below their age-level. (Thus, Patrick, a highly intelligent child of ten who had never attended school and never learnt to read, could be regarded as educationally subnormal, and in need of special educational treatment.) Compared with the pre-1944 position, the categories involved may be tabulated as follows:

1. Those with I.Q.'s between 50 and 70. These children, prior to 1944, would have been classed as 'educable feeble-minded', and could have attended special schools for the mentally defective.
2. Dull children with I.Q.'s between 70 and 80.

3. Those of *any* I.Q. whose attainments are lower than 80 per cent of their age.

Categories 2 and 3 are new, and it is their addition which so greatly increases the number of children who are subject to be dealt with. It is a great merit of the 1944 Act that it makes it possible to provide special help for a very large number of children, who would not have come within the scope of a narrower definition, and that it makes for greater flexibility of administration.

But this greater flexibility is bought at a price. On the one side there is the possibility of confusion among parents, teachers, and the general public if they simply equate 'educationally subnormal' with 'mentally defective', ignoring the very considerable differences, and it is important that teachers at least should be completely clear in their minds that a boy may be educationally subnormal and yet rightly retained in the ordinary school. On the other hand, it is paradoxically easier rather than harder for a careless Local Authority to sidestep its obligations with regard to ascertainment. Prior to 1944 the transfer to a M.D. school of Charlie who was a nuisance, but whose intelligence quotient was relatively high, could be challenged on the ground that he was not mentally defective, but now (unless the circumstances were quite exceptional) he would be fairly sure to come under the wide E.S.N. umbrella. It is excellent that Charlie's need for special help is recognised, but at the same time it is easy to fill the special E.S.N. schools with Charlies and then for the Authority to sit back complacently and do nothing about other children whose need is greater. The point is, that the wide definition of educational subnormality could be made to cover 10 to 15 per cent of the total school population, and that under no conceivable circumstances are there likely to be special schools for anything approaching that number: 1 per cent is probably the limit of practicability, i.e. a small fraction of the total number of possible candidates.

It therefore becomes a matter of considerable practical importance how this proportion is selected. The question is not so much, 'Would this boy profit from the special opportunities that the special school provides?' (it could probably be answered affirmatively for many children), as 'How do this boy's needs compare with those of other children, many of whom have not been brought to the notice of the Authority? Of the available places, how can they best be allocated?' The matter would be simple if the fact that children had not been brought to the notice of the Authority meant that there was no need for them to be brought, and although many Authorities do in practice make that comfortable assumption, yet it is one which has little foundation in reality. It is a common experience that just to scratch the surface in many primary or secondary modern schools reveals children of similar calibre to those in the E.S.N. schools, and that the population of the special schools could be paralleled many times over from the ordinary schools of the district. This statement can be substantiated both by theoretical expectation and by the experience of surveys. Take the theoretical evidence first. In an average neighbourhood one would expect to find 1 to 2 per cent of the entire school population with an I.Q. below 70, and 8 or 10 per cent in addition with I.Q.'s between 70 and 80: if therefore a borough with 30,000 children wished to make provision for only the most handicapped of its children, those with I.Q.'s below 70, it would need about 500 places, and if it wished to make additional provision also for the most difficult of those in the 'dull' group (Category 2) it would need well over 2,000 places. It is true that these need not necessarily be in special schools, yet provision on the scale required to comply entirely with the Ministry's suggestions is very rarely found in any Authority. The usual provision for an area of the size given is more likely to be in the neighbourhood of 200 special school places, of which as many as half may be taken up by Categories

2 and 3, yet even to deal fully with Category 1, which is after all the prime function of the special E.S.N. schools, would require more than twice as many. It may be objected that mere I.Q. level is not the sole determinant. That is true, and the question of the criteria to be used in special school selection will need further consideration, but my point here is that on I Q. alone, the scale of ascertainment is demonstrably insufficient, and that even if we add those who are waiting for special school places the total does not nearly approach the expected level of ascertainment. (If other considerations were included as well, the anticipated numbers would rise still further.)

The national position[1] is:

Attending special E.S.N. schools	22,639
Awaiting places in „ „	12,578
Total	35,217

This out of a total school population of over six and a half million is rather over 0·5 per cent.

Turning now to recent surveys, the same picture is to be seen.[2]

In 1953, in a borough with a school population (ages four to eleven) of between 21,000 and 22,000, 102 children of the same primary ages were attending its special E.S.N. school. Of these 102, 40 were ex-borough pupils, but 3 borough children were in outside E.S.N. schools, making a total of 65 of the borough's children in E.S.N. schools, i.e. about 0·3 per cent. Furthermore, the I.Q. analysis was:

Below 50	50-59	60-69	70-79	80-89	90 +
9	20	38	30	4	1

[1] *Education in 1955*, H.M.S.O. Cmd. 9785, Tables 44 and 51.
[2] Unpublished surveys by Mr R. B. Lendon and Mrs E. D. Farrelly. I am grateful to them and to the Local Education Authorities concerned for permission to use this material.

B

Without pressing the figures too rigidly, it would appear probable that some of the lower ones may ultimately prove to be ineducable, and some of the higher ones belong to Categories 2 and 3; just over half appear to be in Category 1 (educable mentally handicapped children). The proportion receiving special education given above, 0·3 per cent, should therefore be cut down accordingly if account is taken only of Category 1.

Finally, enquiry in the ordinary primary schools suggested that 'a number of children who ought to be ascertained, and

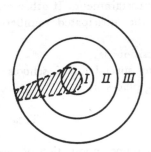

who would benefit from a course of special treatment in the E.S.N. schools, were . . . retained in the ordinary schools. . . . . there is a need for more special school provision, and also a need to combat the stigma that still attaches to these schools.'

In another district, a post-war estate of 3,096 children (ages five to fifteen), 22 children had been ascertained, 16 of them with I.Q.'s above 70, and only 6 below. Eight children (not by any means those whose intelligences were lowest) were attending special E.S.N. schools outside the area, and the remainder attended ordinary schools. It is fair to point out that the rapid expansion of the district had posed great problems in the provision of any sort of education, and not unnaturally the question of providing for deviant children had had to wait, but it does suggest that further enquiry would soon reveal other mentally handicapped children beside the 6 who had actually been ascertained.

These were from districts within Greater London and are unlikely to be improved upon in rural areas where difficulties of ascertainment and provision of special educational treatment are in any case greater.

The position may be roughly expressed in diagram form as follows:

Total area (I+II+III)= 10 to 15 per cent of *all* children.

Inner Circle—I.Q. 50-70.
Middle Ring—I.Q. 70-80.
Outer Ring—Children of any higher intelligence level, whose attainments are lower than 80 per cent of the normal.
Shaded portion—those in E.S.N. schools.

Notes:

1. All these children are, technically, educationally subnormal.

2. A small proportion only is in E.S.N. schools.

3. Those in E.S.N. schools include some whose handicap is less grave (II and III): but they do not include *all* the most seriously handicapped children (I).

4. The whole group requires special educational treatment of one form or another.

It is difficult to resist the conclusion that ascertainment is a chancy business and rather resembles a boy fishing for tiddlers with a jar. He fills his jar, as the Authorities fill their schools, and goes away content: but they are not by any means the only, and may not be the biggest, tiddlers, and the rest remain untroubled in their pools. It is unsatisfactory that a child's chances of getting the special help he needs should depend so largely on extraneous factors such as the district in which he lives, the school which he attends (some schools regularly refer children for examination, others rarely or never) and even his own conduct. If ascertainment were less sporadic and more even, I believe that the sheer size of the problem which is still largely unrecognised by many Authorities would be revealed, and in this sense, more adequate ascertainment is the key to the whole question of the provision of special educational treatment. Were the extent of the need realised, not only would there be demand for more special school places, but Authorities would be in a better position to cut their coat according to their cloth, and make better use of existing places. At present it is all too easy to criticise both the choice of children who are in E.S.N. schools and the large number of the disinherited, who never get a chance of special education at all.

Why is it that ascertainment should be so uneven? It depends on the initiative of parents and Head Teachers in bringing children forward for examination, but in many cases, they are unwilling to act and nothing is done. The reluctance of parents is understandable, but Head Teachers should be in a position to take a more balanced view. In the old days transfer to a special school was thought to carry a stigma, and tradition dies hard; but a more reasonable attitude at the present time would be to stress the benefit to the child which attendance at a special school should bring. It is true that there are bad special schools just as there are bad primary and modern and grammar schools, but it would be just as unwise to condemn all special schools for that reason as it would be to condemn all grammar schools. If a child is not learning in the ordinary school (or learning only that he is a failure) it is far kinder to him to refer him for examination so that at least official attention is called to his un-met needs. He may or may not be transferred to another school, but anyway the Authority is made aware of his existence. To fail to refer these children is to condemn both them and their class teacher to continued frustration, and to hamper the Authority in its efforts to provide adequately for its handicapped pupils.

In an area where provision is known to be inadequate and the likelihood of action remote, Head Teachers are tempted to become cynical and refrain from referral on the grounds that it is useless 'for nothing ever happens'. Yet that is simply to perpetuate the vicious circle, and it can only be broken when the full extent of the hidden need is made plain.

I would like to conclude this section by describing a plan for systematic ascertainment which worked successfully in one area for some years and which avoids the unevenness and waste which results when referral is left largely to chance. The main features of the plan were (1) the initiative came from the Education Office and did not depend on the varying standards of a number of Head Teachers, (2) the area of search was delimited by choosing one age group and sticking to that, rather than disseminating effort over every child of school age. An officer of the Authority—in this case the Educational Psychologist— visited each junior school every year, and discussed with the Head Teacher all the very dull children in one age-group (in this case the seven to eight year group), including those who happened to be absent at the time of the visit. A rapid screening procedure reduced the number who needed full examination to manageable limits and in this way a large number of children could be covered without fuss, without undue expenditure of time and with a reasonable certainty that the full extent of the children needing special educational treatment was being revealed. The actual ascertainment was carried out in the usual way in the Education Office in the presence of the parent, but the preliminary investigations in the schools had several advantages. Not only were they reasonably complete and economical of time, but they were welcomed by the Head Teachers. Head Teachers who would rarely, if ever, refer children for statutory examination if left to themselves, were very ready to co-operate when approached in this way. Furthermore, the quiet slow child who is often missed by the usual procedure as the extent of his backwardness is unrealised because he does not call attention to himself could be detected and helped. In this way a balance could be kept between the needs of all types of children, and the timid and retreating as well as the aggressive and delinquent were brought into consideration. A final advantage was that the Authority was in possession of a fairly complete picture of the whole situation, not only as regards children who needed to be sent to an E.S.N. school, but also as regards others who were likely to need special educational treatment, the dull and backward, and those with behaviour problems; and so was able to plan accordingly. I have advocated elsewhere[1] the desirability of Child Guidance personnel going frequently into the schools in order to discover children with emotional difficulties instead of waiting for them to be referred or not referred more or less haphazardly; and the same applies where educational needs are concerned. It is only in the schools that the full extent of the problem is seen. Then too, Head Teachers are more likely to discuss their children informally with a visitor on the spot, be he psychologist, nurse, or Care Committee worker, than they are to take the more formal step of writing to an impersonal office or clinic.

A scheme of this nature would be useful for those Authorities who are starting new special schools. Presumably the nucleus of the school would be formed from those children already known to the Authority (with the proviso that they should be freshly re-examined, and not simply admitted from a waiting list which may have been compiled some years before), but as the school becomes established and able to take in more children, new admissions should enter at the bottom in an orderly sequence.

[1] In my book *Psychology in the Service of the School.*

It is worth noting from all this that ascertainment is not just a matter of collecting names for a special school, but is a means of discovering the range and extent of the need, so that the Authority is in a position to find out what forms of provision (in the plural, note, not special schools only) are required. It is true that formal ascertainment of a particular child is required only when administrative action, such as transfer to a special school, is contemplated, but it would be a mistake to think of ascertainment entirely in special school terms. We need to distinguish between the two senses of the word: (1) ascertainment of a child, preceding his receiving special educational treatment, and (2) ascertainment from the Local Authority's point of view, when it discovers (or ascertains) the size of the problem. It is in this second sense that ascertainment is so often rather sketchily carried out, and which I have been dealing with up to the present. In what follows I shall be dealing mainly with ascertainment in the first sense. I turn now to consider matters that are taken into account in considering the transfer of a child to a special school.

I. AGE

It is universally agreed that if a child is to profit from special school education, he should not start on it too late. Although many examples can be given of children entering E.S.N. schools for the first time at thirteen or fourteen, there is nothing whatever to commend the practice. The children are old enough to feel shame and resentment at the transfer and are often troublesome, and even though a skilful and patient teacher may eventually win them round, that is no justification. Such a skilful and patient teacher could have done more, had he had them earlier. Prior to 1944 it could be argued—weakly, I think, but still with some point—that a late transfer could be justified since only so could the adolescent be given necessary supervision after leaving. Cases were known of boys and girls being transferred to the special school within a week or two of reaching school leaving age because, had they left from the ordinary school (however low their mental level), they could not be notified to the Mental Deficiency Committee as they were not 'subject to be dealt with' under the Mental Deficiency Acts unless and until they committed an offence. This was particularly true of girls who were out of hand and in need of protection, which could only be given under the Mental Deficiency Acts had they actually left from an M.D. school. But even this shred of justification is now removed, for providing certain conditions are complied with, it is now possible for a boy or girl to be reported to the Mental Health Committee, having left from an ordinary school. These conditions are that he should have been registered as a handicapped pupil receiving special educational treatment, and it is important that teachers should be aware of the possibility, and should find out the administrative procedure to be followed in their own district in order to take advantage of this. It is particularly useful in rural areas where, owing to the difficulty of setting up special schools, it often happens that a child whom everyone knows to be mentally handicapped remains in the ordinary school.

Children are often 'discovered' for the first time at the secondary selection examination or when they enter a secondary modern school. In many people's opinion, this is still far too late, and the practice of transferring senior children to E.S.N. schools should cease, and they should instead be given special educational treatment in ordinary schools. It is argued that they cannot be the worst cases (otherwise they would have been picked out earlier) and that having demonstrated their ability to keep their head above water to the age of eleven, they should be allowed to remain. The weakness of this position is that they might quite well be bad cases, and one cannot argue that because they have been overlooked for six years, therefore they should be neglected for another four. This, however, is not at all what is intended, if the provisions for special educational treatment in the modern school are satisfactory. It is useless to connive at six years' neglect by allowing such children to enter the E.S.N. school far too late: what is needed is to cut at the root of the neglect by ensuring (e.g. on the lines suggested earlier) that it cannot occur.

A possible exception to this occurs in the case of rural areas whose special schools must be residential. There are many difficulties in the way of providing residential places for quite young children, and parents' opposition to special schools is likely to be increased if it means being away from home. It is arguable that the disadvantage to a child under eleven of being away from an ordinarily good home outweighs any *educational* advantages that he can gain from being in the special school rather than the village school. Hence country authorities have tended quite reasonably to concentrate their provision of special residential schools on those over eleven (except for those younger children who have no home or who need to be removed from home—but that is a different problem).

With this exception, however, it is desirable that children who need to go to special schools should go by the age of eight or nine, certainly not later than ten. But how early should they be picked out? Is there a lower limit below which it is undesirable to send children into special E.S.N. schools?

Under the 1944 Act it is possible for children to be ascertained from two onwards, but in practice (with the exception of obviously handicapped children who are likely to be ineducable) few are discovered before the age of five. Some authorities do not admit children to their special schools before the age of seven or eight; others will take them as young as five into classes which are run on nursery lines. In favour of early admissions, it is argued that children do not have the experience of failure, though when this argument is put forward by those Authorities who at the same time are prepared to countenance very late transfers, it seems a little odd. In opposition to this, it is very difficult with young children to be sure of the accuracy of estimates of ability. Quite obviously, none of these children have had much chance to prove themselves in the ordinary school, and so the evidence of lack of response to the opportunities the school provides is missing. That means that all the weight has to be placed on mental tests and on social and emotional characteristics. But the variability of response in young children makes accurate testing difficult. They may or may not co-operate: they may be distracted by a strange situation and a strange tester: they may be shy or inarticulate or hampered by an untreated sensory or speech defect. These difficulties apply at all ages, but they are greatest with younger children. Then it has to be remembered that the younger the child, the greater the difference that a few months of Mental Age makes in arriving at an I.Q.—the margin of safety is less at a time when the chance of error is particularly great. The estimate of subnormality in a five-year-old involves a very difficult double diagnosis—between ineducability on the one hand and mere dullness on the other—and I for one would not care to make it with any certainty, bearing in mind that it is an important decision to make in the life of a child, and that the likelihood of error is high. Furthermore, social and emotional characteristics can be very misleading. An untrained child, who flies into a tantrum or wets on the examiner's floor or rushes distractibly round the room, creates a poor impression; so does one who has never been allowed to use his hands and is helpless with coat and buttons, but all these, while they may be signs of defective intelligence, may also be attributable to faults of parental handling.

These theoretical doubts are confirmed when one considers the children in actual attendance at an E.S.N. nursery class. A high proportion, as one would expect, are probable ineducables who are in 'on trial', but of the remainder there are too many who are misfits for opposite reasons. For instance, Ruth was sent to the E.S.N. school shortly after her fifth birthday. Soon after she was six she was recognising flash cards and calling on all and sundry to hear her. The teacher was pardonably proud of her success, but less pardonably anxious to retain her. It is understandable that she should like to have her in her class, for she was a docile and friendly child as well as responsive, but after all, there is the child to be considered—and also all the other children who need special education and are not getting it. At the time when this occurred the district was badly in need of provisions for special education, and it is difficult to defend her retention.

However careful the examining doctor, frequent mistaken assessments are bound to occur, simply because the conditions are so favourable to error. In the great majority of cases, it would seem preferable to retain children in the infant schools and let them have a fair trial for two years there instead of prematurely ascertaining them. Teachers in infant schools, when asked for their opinion, are usually willing to retain such children (provided, of course, that they are not grossly and patently defective—in which case they should be excluded. It is only where reasonable doubt as to their educability exists that a trial period is recommended by the Ministry.) Infant teachers will often give examples from their experience in which their original judgment on a child's capabilities proved to be astray, and the child developed more than they would have thought possible so that by the age of seven there was no need to consider special school transfer, but even if this does not happen, his capacity can be more accurately gauged when he is older and has had normal chances of learning for two years.

Much, of course, depends on the atmosphere and attitude of the teachers in the actual infant schools under consideration. While even a borderline child can be happily occupied in learning at his own level in a school with a modern approach, the same child could be made miserable by over-pressure. Nothing is gained by keeping him in an environment where all he learns is that he cannot do what other children do. This seems to me a travesty of a description of the average infants school, but where, exceptionally, it holds then there is a case for earlier transfer to the special school. In general, however, the balance of advantage lies with the infants school.

The position changes, however, with the increasing demands of an academic nature that are made on subnormal children in the junior school, and each year that passes renders them more likely to fail, with all the undesirable emotional concomitants that failure entails. The sooner they can receive the special education they need, the better for them, for their junior teachers, for the other children in the (probably large) class, and for the teachers in the special school which finally admits them.

I conclude, therefore, that with rare exceptions children should be admitted to day special E.S.N. schools not earlier than seven and not later than nine or ten. The places saved by not admitting children before seven or eight could well be used for the other children that a more careful and systematic ascertainment would quickly reveal. I cannot think that it is any hardship to Stanley, who is genuinely educationally subnormal, to admit him to the special school at seven or eight instead of five, when one thinks of the numerous Stanleys who as things are do not get their chance at all.

II. INTELLIGENCE

When all is said and done, the main reason for children to be transferred to an E.S.N. school is because they are such slow learners that they need special methods to help them to learn, and therefore in the last resort the I.Q. is probably the crucial criterion in determining transfer to an E.S.N. school.

But having said that, there are at once provisos to be made. The best intelligence tests are delicate and sensitive instruments and need considerable skill in administration and interpretation, not sausage machines into which one feeds a child at one end and receives an I.Q. at the other. Because they are sensitive they are liable to upset—by illness, undetected sensory weakness,[1] a failure in rapport, or other chance disturbances—as well as by sheer errors in timing, scoring, or arithmetic which, human nature being what it is, cannot be ruled out. Futhermore, different tests do not necessarily test the same abilities, and they may have different standard deviations, so that one test cannot be directly compared with another. For all these reasons, whether due to variations in the test, the tester, or the child, the results are likely to fluctuate from one occasion to another. It would be as foolish to deny this as it would be to overestimate it. In many cases, the fluctuations are small, but even where they are larger, it is still fair to say that intelligence tests give the best single estimate of the general mental level of the child in comparison with the rest of the population. It is unnecessary to split hairs as to whether the 'true' I.Q. is 85 or 87 or 81, but at least there is no suggestion that the child is above average or that he is seriously subnormal: the results give an approximate idea of his mental calibre (and hence the type of educational pabulum he needs) but not an exact figure on which anyone should take a stand.

To say that usually children with I.Q.'s below 70 are best in special schools, does not mean that this should be interpreted as a rigid borderline because other factors have to be taken into consideration and besides, as we have seen, the figure itself is subject to fluctuation; but it does suggest certain limits or categories about which certain general statements can be made. In general, children of less than half the normal intelligence

[1] The spuriously low I.Q. which Ruth in the preceding section was given on her original test was largely due to eye trouble which was corrected by glasses after she entered the E.S.N. school.

are likely to prove ineducable. Children of between half and three-quarters the normal intelligence are usually best helped by attending special schools, though there may be exceptions to this . . . and so on. In this way, one can avoid the difficulties which come from untenably rigid borderlines. Nevertheless, even though there is bound to be some overlapping when the other criteria to be discussed later are taken into account, other things being equal those whose intelligence is lowest are those whose need of special school placement is greatest. It is difficult to defend the retention of pupils of relatively high intelligence (say, over 80 I.Q.) in E.S.N. schools, as long as there are *any* in the ordinary schools who are very much lower—say below 65.

Evidence as to the degree to which factors other than low intelligence enter into special school selection comes from a consideration of the sex ratio. It is a common experience in E.S.N. schools that boys greatly outnumber girls, yet were intelligence alone the determinant one would expect to find very little difference. Boys vary more than girls from an average which is similar for both sexes, and that means that one can expect to find more very bright and very dull boys than girls— but the difference is slight and certainly would not account for the heavy preponderance of boys which is found in practice. The excess over expectation is almost certainly to be explained in other ways—by a greater readiness of Head Teachers to refer boys for statutory examination. A boy who finds school work beyond him is less likely than an equally dull girl to 'just sit'—he is more likely to become a nuisance and so call attention to himself, and thereby enter the special school. A girl who sits quietly, even though she is learning nothing, may escape scrutiny throughout the junior school and so remain—but it may be very different when she reaches adolescence, and hence the late referrals of girls which were adversely criticised in the preceding section.

I would go so far as to suggest that the sex ratio forms a good rough guide as to the adequacy with which ascertainment is carried out in an area. If there is a great excess of boys over girls we can be fairly sure that it is inadequate—there is likely to be a hidden reservoir of girls of equally low intelligence who have remained undiscovered and unhelped.

III. ATTAINMENTS

These can be quickly dealt with. A child's lack of attainments is one of the first things to call attention to him. Attainment tests are easily administered, and provide an objective measure of what he has learned or failed to learn. When enquiries are made, they provide the first sieve. Yet their simplicity and objectivity may prove dangerous, if too much weight is attached to their results. There are many reasons why children fail to learn, and low intelligence is only one. If we believe that special schools should in the main cater for those whose handicap is inborn and unalterable and whose need is permanent, we shall pay more attention to the results of intelligence tests than we do to school failure, however glaring. It is true that this calls for a remedy, and that special educational treatment is obviously indicated, but many people would say that the answer is not to be found in taking the drastic step of sending non-readers to the special E.S.N. school, unless they were also qualified on other grounds, e.g. by low intelligence.

It is worth noting in this connection that examining medical officers are not always in a good position to judge the *educational* standing of a child. An example will illustrate the point. A doctor was prepared to recommend a boy whom he had just examined for the special school, although his intelligence was higher than the usual borderline—'after all', he said, 'he's nearly 7 and he can't read a word'. A colleague replied that that was not as unusual as he appeared to suppose and suggested that he should visit 'X' Infant school (in a poor area) from which the boy had come, and see what the rest of the children were like. He did so—and reported in amazement on his return that he had seen a whole class of similar non-readers. Nothing more was heard of the proposed special school transfer. His standards of comparison as to what could be expected of six-year-olds were too high, drawn as they were from the knowledge of what his own son and daughter (favoured both in endowment and environment) could do at that age.

It is often stated that boys are more often backward in reading, and girls in arithmetic. Up to a point this provides a reason for the more frequent referral of boys for statutory examination, as failure in reading is commonly given more weight than failure in arithmetic by Head Teachers who are considering whether or not to bring a child forward. Nevertheless, it does not account for the great disproportion often found, and to explain this we are forced back on to questions of behaviour.

IV. SOCIAL AND EMOTIONAL CHARACTERISTICS

Everyone knows that in practice behaviour is often the chief factor which determines a Head Teacher's decision to refer a child for statutory examination, but the question we are concerned with here is whether this emphasis on behaviour is justifiable.

If the special school is intended primarily to help those who find learning difficult is it not a misuse of its places to fill them with children who are primarily behaviour problems? It is understandable that teachers in the ordinary schools should be more ready to get rid of troublesome children than of quiet ones, and if one thinks of the special school merely as a limbo to which undesirables of all kinds can be consigned, then the practice can be defended. It is probable that the early special schools were so conceived, as receptacles for a mixed and heterogeneous collection of children who were unwelcome in the

24

ordinary schools, for whatever reason. But if the needs of the children are given first place in our consideration, it is surely those children who have greatest difficulty in learning who should attend the special E.S.N. school, because that is the place which provides an education suited to their needs. If we take the word 'special' seriously, the E.S.N. school ceases to be regarded as a dumping ground for misfits, and is considered a place which gives special help *to those who most need its care*.

But here it may be replied that children whose behaviour is unsatisfactory often do have 'great difficulty in learning'. Lowish intelligence, poor attainments, and lack of interest in school pursuits with consequent inattention and misbehaviour form a nexus which it is very difficult to separate out into its constituent elements. Granted that this is so, it is usually possible to distinguish between (1) those in whom the low intelligence is primary and who are 'naughty' because the ordinary school does not and never can meet their needs, and (2) those who are troublesome and fail in school as a result. In the second case the misbehaviour is a cause and in the first a consequence, of school failure: in the first case the failure is inevitable, but in the second case it is not.

If, therefore, we treat causes and not just symptoms, we will try to provide a more suitable type of education, e.g. in a special E.S.N. school, for the first group, but the second group needs further study into the reasons *why* they are troublesome—reasons which may have very little to do with the school, but stem chiefly from the child's personality and home. They too, need special educational treatment, but it is of a kind different from that which the innately mentally handicapped need, and in certain circumstances they may have to be ascertained as maladjusted. Whether such children ought to be sent to an E.S.N. school is much debated: if they are sufficiently backward in school attainments they do come under the wide 'E.S.N.' umbrella, and an Authority can keep within the letter of the law by sending them there, but nevertheless the wisdom of the practice is much to be questioned. We can ask two fundamental questions:

1. How effectively can the E.S.N. school help these children? Is it the right place for them?
2. Whose places are they taking?

In so far as the classes in E.S.N. schools are small and individual attention is possible, the children can be helped more effectively than they could if they remained in the large classes of their previous school. They are probably benefiting more than they would have done in the ordinary school, but that does not mean that the E.S.N. school is the *best* place to meet their needs, for the following reasons:

1. They could move at a quicker pace and respond to a more varied curriculum than the majority of educationally subnormal children to whom the school is rightly geared.

2. Their influence on the other children is not always desirable. In an ordinary school, there are other able children to act as a counterweight, but in an E.S.N. school where by hypothesis they are the brightest elements, they may lead the others into mischief.

3. Some of these children are delinquents. If it is known that they are attending an E.S.N. school, their subsequent transfer to an Approved School is greatly impeded: yet their prime need may be to be away from their home area.

4. The shorter hours of the special school and longer journeys from home are not always in their interest, as they imply more unsupervised free time.

5. They are more likely than the genuine handicapped pupil to be sensitive to and react unfavourably against, any real or supposed stigma that attendance at an E.S.N. school carries.

6. Transfer to an E.S.N. school as a result of school failure is superficial and does not touch the root of the matter in their

case. More careful examination into the *reasons* for their difficulties is required.

7. Most E.S.N. schools would claim greater success for their efforts with timid and retreating children than with young toughs. The former (who are usually genuinely handicapped) gain in confidence when removed from the hurly-burly of a large school into a slower tempo, whereas the latter may not be helped by becoming too easily cock of the walk. (In one sense, this is merely to say that E.S.N. schools are most helpful in dealing with those whom they were set up to help, which is after all their function.)

We may conclude that it is by no means proven that difficult children are most effectively helped by attendance at an E.S.N. school.

The second question to my mind is crucial, and it can be dealt with briefly. Evidence has been brought forward to show that many children of low intelligence are never ascertained but remain in the ordinary school. Presumably they get by by being unobtrusive—to which two comments can be made:

1. Retreating behaviour as well as aggressive conduct may be a sign that something is wrong.

2. Whether they behave quietly or noisily is really neither here nor there when we are considering the need for *educational* help. If he needs special methods to help him to learn, why should he be denied that help because his conduct is satisfactory? Once we progress beyond the notion that transfer to a special school is a punishment, but think of it instead as an opportunity for giving special help, a better perspective on the whole question can be gained. Perhaps an analogy with other forms of handicap can be useful here. The Head Teacher of a junior school would never hesitate to urge the transfer of an almost totally blind little girl to the place where she can receive the special help she needs—the school for the blind—and it would not occur to him to use her good conduct or her mother's

interest in the child as an argument against the transfer. Why then should the attitude of parents and teachers be different when mental handicap is in question?

We touch here on the question of stigma, to which there is no short answer. In the long run, the only way of getting rid of stigma is by the excellence of the work of the E.S.N. school, so that it really does provide what is implicit in its title, *special* education.

But special education for whom? Not for all and sundry, for those who most need the particular help it has to offer. Our discussion of the criteria to be taken into account in considering which children should be selected for the E.S.N. school leads us back to the overriding importance of the inborn factor of general intelligence. Children who lack intelligence *must* fail in school work and they cannot do without the help of special methods. Those of more ability *may* also fail in school and then they too will require special educational treatment at least for a time; but in allocating places in E.S.N. schools, first priority should be given to those in the first category whose need is greatest, and whose need is permanent.

I conclude, therefore, that school failure and social unacceptability should be taken into account as providing additional evidence of incapacity, but the main weight should be given to the level of general intelligence, in deciding which children, of the large minority who come within the wide limits of the term 'educationally subnormal', should be the small minority selected for special school treatment.

Unless ascertainment is full and thorough, the picture of the situation which the Local Authority holds is likely to be seriously incomplete and unbalanced and therefore the provisions which it makes will be so too.

'Special educational treatment' should include, in addition to special E.S.N. schools for the most handicapped, arrangements for giving appropriate help in the ordinary schools to children whose needs are similar but less severe, and also separate arrangements for dealing with maladjusted children (remembering that these may include withdrawn as well as troublesome children). To expect one institution, the E.S.N. school, to cater for all these different needs in a partial and haphazard way, is to expect the impossible. It is no exaggeration, therefore, to say that the key to the whole question of the proper provision of special educational treatment is to be found in adequate ascertainment.

CHAPTER III

The Organisation of Classes in E.S.N. Schools

M OST E.S.N. schools are small in comparison with ordinary schools. At the beginning of 1955 there were as many as 52 out of a total of 256 E.S.N. schools in England and Wales with fewer than 50 pupils,[1] but the number of very small schools can be expected to diminish as a result of the Ministry's policy, which is not to approve any *new* special schools of less than five classes (all ages) or three (primary or secondary only), and as existing small schools are enlarged as part of an Authority's development plan. Even so, schools of more than 200 pupils are uncommon (the median number on roll in January 1954 was between 75 and 100). Apart from considerations of expediency which limit the size of special schools in comparison with ordinary schools (for instance, the need to keep the catchment area within manageable travelling distance) it is often held as a point of principle that the children attending them flourish best in a small community where they can be genuinely seen as individuals.

The typical E.S.N. school probably has five or six classes with which to cater for an age range that may be six to sixteen, with the upper part of the school top heavy as more children are discovered towards the end of their school life. It is rare to find a class with only one age group and not uncommon to find a range of three or four chronological years in the one class. This

[1] *Education in 1955*, Table 50.

is in marked contrast to the usual urban junior or secondary school where there are enough children of one age group to fill several classes and three or four streams are common. It is true that the range of ability is very much less but even so it has to be remembered that the restricted range of ability may still be accompanied by very great discrepancies in attainment level. A group of fifteen-year-old boys, for instance, even though the I.Q. range may be no more than 20 points, may vary all the way in Reading Age from nil to as much as twelve or thirteen years, and nearly as great a spread (differently constituted) may be found in Arithmetic. Additional complications are caused by marked variations in social and emotional development, in physical maturity and in the possession of special talents and disabilities.

To this may often be added (if the school is a mixed one) a marked disproportion in the numbers of boys and girls with consequent difficulty in arranging for practical subjects. One E.S.N. school, for example, an all age mixed school, larger than most, received at the age of eleven the *boys* from two other E.S.N. schools (the girls remaining in their original schools). In addition to these transfers there were, of course, their own boys and girls, so that the senior classes had a sex ratio of about five to one. At each stage (note: not each age-group— each class contained two years and the five years from eleven to sixteen were covered in three stages) there were three parallel classes, two of boys and one mixed. There were only enough girls to make half a class three times over and hence the stage system had to be retained and every class contained a mixture of age groups, with all the complications that this entails. It is true that this is not a typical example, but it does show the difficulties of organisation that may arise.

It may be said that some of the difficulties of organisation are not inevitable, but are the results of an unwise admissions policy, and could be avoided by more systematic ascertainment on the lines advocated in the previous chapter, and by balancing the sex ratio. Or again, if a number of children of rather higher abilities be sent to the E.S.N. school the range of mental age in any one class may widen out unmanageably. One way to get rid of this is to promote the abler children to a higher class—but the discrepancy then reappears in the form of a wide variation in *chronological* ages within the one class, heterogeneity in social development and so on. Furthermore, these abler children are presumably markedly lacking in scholastic attainments, since otherwise (with their greater ability) why should they have been sent to the E.S.N. school at all? It is by no means certain that they can adapt themselves well in the higher class. The only other way is by adopting some sort of streaming—and this raises further issues which need to be examined.

Until recently, streaming was very rarely to be met in E.S.N. schools, with the exception of one or two of the largest. If a school contains enough children of similar age to form more than one class (as in ordinary schools and a few very large special schools) little surprise can be expressed if the classes are made more homogeneous by some sort of ability/attainment grouping, i.e. by streaming. But if the attempt is made to stream in a much smaller school, it does become surprising and one begins to wonder *why* it is done. It is obvious that two streams can be achieved only by increasing the chronological age range in each class and where this is already high, considerable unwieldiness results. If a primary E.S.N. school, for instance, with five classes to cater for a five to eleven age range runs them 'straight' with a reasonable amount of overlapping to cover the inevitable unevennesses of development, and the children work on individual lines, a fairly comprehensible picture results. But if a similar school were to be organised so that children on leaving the admission class at seven were divided into two streams (on what evidence, one wonders? for that age is a very early one for educationally subnormal children, and no signs of 'progress' in the formal sense are to be expected) it is difficult to see what advantage is gained as presumably the children would be working individually in any case (or would they?). Homogeneity of grouping in the ordinary school with its very wide range of abilities is advocated to make it easier to deal with large numbers by class methods, and this does not—or should not—apply in the special school. Furthermore, five-year-old entrants to the Infant school are not streamed, and this corresponds to an age of seven or eight in the E.S.N. school. With older special school children of secondary age, somewhat different considerations apply, the main one being the extreme variability of performance of the same child in different branches of school work, so that streaming has little adequacy. Only a multitude of cross-classifications could really serve here, and this has disadvantages of its own. I did hear of one E.S.N. school where, with ruthless logic, the boys were divided into different 'sets' for every conceivable subject: but as this made even a visitor's head whirl, one can imagine that it was chaotically incomprehensible to the boys themselves, and the very antithesis of what one hopes for educationally subnormal children in the way of providing a steady and stable environment.

I am inclined to think that some of the attraction of streaming comes from pretending that it is an ordinary school. The modern school is streamed and therefore the E.S.N. school tries to copy it, just as the modern school too often apes the grammar school irrespective of the suitability of the model. If only it had the courage to be itself! I have tried to show that conditions are so different between the two sets of schools that copying is inappropriate. Again, it is worth noting that the value of streaming in ordinary schools is becoming questioned. We have no need to enter into that controversy, but whatever the merits or demerits of streaming in ordinary schools at least the conditions there are far more favourable to streaming than they are in special schools.

A further attraction of streaming may be that it is thought to help in the 'de-ascertainment' of selected children. This is a question which will need full examination on its own, and so will only be mentioned here.

One further objection to streaming seems to me final. This is that it can so easily become associated with the very antithesis of all that the special school stands or should stand for—the philosophy of 'the weakest to the wall'. Many people criticise the ordinary school for paying too little attention to the needs of its weaker members. If this is a fault, then at least the special school should be free of it, by its very terms of reference. In an ordinary school, the needs of dull children have to be weighed against the needs of the normal and bright, and due attention given to each. It is said to be a particular merit of a special school that it is free from such conflicting claims and that each child should be considered in his own right. The competitive attitudes and pressures for results of the ordinary school should have no place in the special school.

Sometimes complaints are made that there are schools where the A streams have an undue share of equipment and stock, and the B streams make do with what is left. This is hard to defend in ordinary schools, and for special schools it would be indefensible. Much the same applies in the allocation of teachers to the different classes. It is still too frequently a point of honour with successful teachers that they should be assigned to successful classes, but in the ordinary school there is at least some justification for this practice. In the special school there is none. It will be a bad day for the special school movement if ever it gets about that one class, and hence its teacher, is 'better' than another class. Wherever the post of honour and special responsibility is in an ordinary school, in an E.S.N. school it is with the weakest and the slowest children, otherwise it will forfeit whatever moral authority it possesses.

I conclude that streaming in the special school raises more problems than it solves in organisation, and is undesirable in principle. In any case, a more careful admission policy on the part of Local Authorities could go far to obviate the need if the range of ability was kept within manageable limits.

So far it has been possible to discuss together a number of factors which complicate the organisation of classes in E.S.N. schools. It has been suggested that some of these could be avoided while others stem from the nature of the case.

There is one overriding difficulty which is so important that a general discussion will not serve and it must be considered separately.

That is, that the population of special schools is constantly shifting. Transfers can be effected at any time, and are liable to affect every class in the school, since if several children are admitted at the bottom other children must move up to make room for them, and so on. The drawbacks of this procedure are obvious, both socially and educationally. It is important to any child and particularly so to an educationally subnormal child, to belong to a small stable social unit, with which he can identify himself, but it is difficult to do this when the members of that unit change at frequent intervals. He may be doing much of his work, in the basic subjects for instance, on individual lines, but group activities are also an essential part of his development. Group projects are impeded if 'general post' is the order of the day. Each single child probably stays with the same teacher for a considerable time—perhaps two or three years—but the class is continually changing. It is the sort of system which can work at all only if the pattern of the school is very flexible, but it imposes a particularly heavy responsibility on the teachers without being to the advantage of the children.

Flexibility of organisation is all very well, but too much fluidity can easily spill over into shapelessness and the drift of laissez-faire unless *all* the following conditions are fulfilled: (1) the staff work closely together, (2) really careful and adequate records are kept of each child, and maintained up to date at all times, (3) every single teacher is an excellent organiser able to make 'individual work' into a reality and not just a pious shibboleth, (4) measures are taken of set policy, to give the children a feeling of belonging to a stable unit. It rarely happens that all these conditions are fulfilled together, particularly when one thinks of the difficulty of staffing some E.S.N. schools at all. As long as it persists, it presents the less zealous teachers with a gratuitous excuse for failure to look ahead and do even the most necessary planning and preparation.

These remarks apply particularly to those schools where children may be admitted at any time, and the classes alter more frequently than once a term. Other schools are reorganised every term, which is bad enough, but less bad than the foregoing. There are finally a few where a studied attempt has been made to evolve a settled framework which will stand for a year, as in ordinary schools, and it may be useful to describe these in detail.

One school has been granted permission to start the year in September with an exceptionally small admission class. The other classes are up to full strength, even (in the case of the top class) overfull, as some children will reach sixteen and leave during the year, leaving eventually a rather small class, but nevertheless it will not be added to. The teachers agreed that, in spite of the apparent inequalities to begin with, it would be worth their while to keep the same group unchanged through the year. All the movement will take place into one class, where it is felt that gradual admissions will be helpful as it will give each new entrant a chance to find his feet in turn. This experiment will be watched with interest and so far seems to be working well, but it will be some time before it is possible to judge its success.

The crucial question is whether *all* admissions can suitably be allocated to the lowest class. As the school is one for seniors only, the main body of entrants (those leaving the primary E.S.N. school which feeds this) is known in advance, but the plan can succeed only if stray transfers on a large and unpredictable scale from secondary modern schools are discouraged, and especially if much older boys and girls, who could not well be placed in the bottom class, are not sent. That, of course, would be all to the good.

Another sort of stabilisation concerns an all age school, where the Authority adopted a policy of systematic ascertainment on the lines described in the previous chapter. It will be remembered that all children during their first year in the junior school were examined as necessary, and a list of priorities established. Those who needed to go to the special school were admitted *en bloc* in the following September, i.e. at the beginning of their second junior year, and no further transfers took place until the following September, except where families had moved into the district from another area. In this way the special school approximated to the practice of ordinary schools: the number and names of children who would be entering the school were known in advance and necessary contacts could be made with the schools from which the children were coming and information collected and the classes could be as stable as those in ordinary schools apart from the inevitable sporadic transfer from another district. At the same time the Heads of the junior schools knew beforehand who would be going, and also, and more important, who would *not* be going. If John was not admitted to the E.S.N. school at the age of eight, his Head Teacher knew that he would not go later on either,[1] and so there was no temptation to keep on referring the same child

[1] Save, of course, in really exceptional circumstances.

in the hope that finally importunity would carry the day. Most Heads were glad to know where they stood, and it was also to the advantage of the children in that the responsibility for helping them was fairly and squarely in one place, with no loopholes such as 'perhaps by next term he will have gone, so let us wait and see what happens'.

It should be noted that when the scheme was first started it involved a certain cutting of losses with regard to older children, but it was felt to be more important to get the system of entry into the special school on a proper footing so that after some years it could be felt that no child whose need was *grave* had been forgotten. Of course, the older children passed over at the start of the scheme and the numerous Johns who each year were considered but not accepted for the special school, needed and were given alternative help. The Authority was in a position to provide special educational treatment for such dull and retarded children, because it had ascertained the extent of the provision likely to be required.

This scheme differs from the last in that the children were admitted as a block rather than gradually absorbed, and also in that it deals with younger children (the exact age of admittance is of course immaterial). Each has merits and demerits, but at least both get rid of the bugbear of frequent changes in class structure. Perhaps it is too much to hope for that yearly promotions should everywhere be established, but at least it is quite unnecessary to have changes more frequently than once a term, and this could be considered a first objective, with yearly promotions a long term but by no means unattainable goal.

Finally, one senior E.S.N. school is running a five-year plan, by which each teacher stays with the same class and moves with it up the school. Obviously, this plan can work only if the staff is stable, and if there is no weak link in the chain; but even though it may never be widely copied, the fact that it can be done at all shows that 'general post' is not necessary.

We may conclude that the conditions which are inescapable are—a range of several years in one class, an even larger scatter in attainment, and hence the need for individual work and careful record keeping. Conditions which are avoidable, or at least mitigable, by a suitable admission policy, are—an unbalanced sex ratio, an unduly wide range of mental age, and constantly changing classes.

Within the framework of the inescapable conditions, that organisation is most likely to be satisfactory which is the simplest. Unduly complicated organisation which may be necessary in a large school can be dispensed with in a small, and in any case it is well to remember that elaborate schemes are incomprehensible to E.S.N. children.

CHAPTER IV

Reorganisation in E.S.N. Schools

THE majority of E.S.N. schools are all-age. In 1955 there were 142 all-age schools, and 114 (40 + 74) divided into primary and secondary.[1] The characteristic picture is of a single day school per authority, containing both sexes and all ages. This holds for all but the largest urban authorities: usually it is only the big cities which provide more than one E.S.N. school, and where any other type of organisation is at all possible.

The following discussion therefore applies only to those authorities which have several E.S.N. day schools within their jurisdiction, and who are free, if they wish, to classify the children attending E.S.N. schools along lines of sex or age.

The arguments in favour of separating primary and secondary departments can be summarised as follows:

1. It has been generally conceded that for the majority of children reorganisation along the lines advocated by the Hadow Report (and assumed as an integral condition in the 1944 Act) is beneficial. In reorganising E.S.N. schools, then, we are simply applying to educationally subnormal children what has already been conceded as desirable for all ordinary children, and bringing them into line with general policy.

2. As a corollary to this, it can be argued that the children will feel themselves singled out as 'different' if their school, unlike the schools their neighbours attend, is an all-age one.

3. Advantageous economies in the provision of equipment

[1] *Education in 1955*, Table 45.

and apparatus result from reorganisation. Where a school of total roll 120 contains, let us say, thirty girls and forty boys of senior age, it is difficult to make adequate provision for practical subjects. The small numbers mean that expensive Domestic Science and Woodwork centres are only in part-time use. This is uneconomical, and when a number of schools have similar needs, the cost and waste of unused facilities becomes great. Attendances of the children at outside centres have their own disadvantages—the time taken in travel, the risk of accidents on the journey, and particularly the separation of the practical work from the rest of the curriculum. Yet the importance of adequate training in practical subjects is beyond question for educationally subnormal children. A tempting solution can be found if the schools in one quarter of the city are grouped together: all the facilities for boys' practical work given to one, and for girls to another, and the others which are to become primary schools, generously provided with nursery-infant equipment. It is undeniable that in this way a far more elaborate standard of material provision can be reached for the same total expenditure.

At the same time, the argument is not all one way, and weighty social and educational considerations can be urged on the other side.

1. It can be said that the experience of the ordinary school is not necessarily relevant. As the E.S.N. school is a *special* school, it need not and should not follow the precedents of ordinary schools in every respect unless it is proved to be to the advantage of the children to do so. Special school children, by the nature of the case, deviate from the ordinary pattern, and if this should prove to be one respect in which their educational needs are different from those of the rest, the question falls.

But, of course, the onus of proof is on those who say that there *is* such a difference in this respect.

2. Similar considerations apply to the question of children's feelings. It is wise to take all reasonable steps to minimise the children's feelings of being 'different', but if they *are* different and can best be helped by a procedure which varies from the normal, what then? If this argument were given unchecked sway, we should not provide E.S.N. schools at all. Presumably, if a child differs so much from the normal that he needs to attend a special school, he is already singled out by his own handicap, and what goes on elsewhere need not be considered— the important thing is to make sure that the education he receives is that best fitted to his needs. Here again, the onus of proof is on those who maintain that this can best be served by departing from the usual pattern.

It is an onus which can only be discharged by an examination of the educational and social factors which are alleged to make this difference, and to these I now turn.

3. A good case can be made for urging that a break at eleven plus is detrimental to an educationally subnormal child's progress in the tool subjects. The break comes at the very time when he may be reaching the quickening point in reading, and before his skill is consolidated. Relatively few children leave the primary E.S.N. school with fluency so well established that it is proof against the shock of transfer to a new environment, and for the rest the transfer comes as a setback. Even where close contact is maintained between the two schools, this is so, and where there is little or no effective liaison, the setback is greater. Examples have been known where children have been changed to an entirely different reading series or, almost worse, put back to one they thought they had outgrown.

Records do not entirely bridge the gap, even when they have been well kept, and when they have not, the gap is all the greater, since the receiving teacher has little to go on about the child's previous work.

Change of school, then, can come as a gratuitous interruption of a child's progress in learning to read and at a particularly vital time.[1]

4. Many teachers in E.S.N. schools urge that if there has to be a break, it should not be at the age of eleven, but later. Here the analogy with normal children is misleading, because whether or not they are then ready for a break, the educationally subnormal child certainly is not. His mental age is then somewhere between six and eight, and to wait until he reaches a mental age of eleven plus one would need to wait until he is fifteen or sixteen, i.e. school leaving age.

5. It should be remembered that many children do not reach the E.S.N. school until they are already nine or ten and where this is so the primary school is faced with a hopeless task as the interval before the child moves on again is impossibly short. They have hardly got to know him, much less to help and train him effectively, before he has to leave. If the task of the primary school is to lay firm foundations on which the secondary school can later build, it should be given reasonable conditions within which to work, and these conditions are not reasonable. They discourage teachers who genuinely wish to get to know the children and encourage a child-minding attitude 'we can't do much, he'll soon have gone elsewhere', which is the very antithesis of what special school treatment should provide.

If an Authority wishes to separate its primary and secondary schools, a precondition for its success is to have a systematic admission policy by which children enter the primary school early enough, and stay long enough to be profitable. As things are, an educationally subnormal child can have had three breaks by the time he is eleven—from infant to junior, from

---

[1] Research is needed at this point, and as far as I am aware, no published evidence is available. The result of a preliminary enquiry by Mr W. E. T. Butler, which reached me after the above was written, does not suggest that transfer is necessarily harmful to reading, but his numbers were small and confined to one school.

junior to E.S.N., and from one E.S.N. department to another—quite apart from any additional changes due to moving house, etc.

6. Continuity is particularly important for educationally subnormal children, more so than for normal children. Steps of learning must be small and carefully graded, and gaps avoided at all costs. Where an average child can fill in the gaps for himself, if they are not too large, and orient himself quickly to new materials and methods, this is liable to be too much for educationally subnormal children, and the elements remain unintegrated and confused in their minds.

7. The same need for continuity is to be found when we turn from scholastic to social and emotional factors. I have already commented on the adverse effect of too frequent changes within classes; and the subnormal child's need for a stable environment is best served by avoiding changes of school if possible. He can be helped more in the slow process of establishing himself and developing an integrated personality if he stays in one school where he is known. It has to be remembered also that educationally subnormal children frequently come from homes where family relationships are defective in one way or another, and where it is very difficult for the children to receive the steady background of training and discipline that they need. If anything, subnormal children are more dependent than other children on a good pattern of habitual conduct, and when this is lacking at home, the school may be the only substitute. Of course, it cannot be a complete substitute, but such as it is, it is better than nothing; and it does appear unwise to interfere with the child's need for continuity in schooling unless there are very pressing and important reasons (as for instance the decision to transfer him to a special school in the first place).

8. From the teacher's point of view, similar considerations apply. Knowledge of children as individuals is only gradually built up over a period of time and much time is wasted when

the new set of teachers in a new school has to get to know him. As with his educational progress, so with his social and emotional development, however full the previous teacher's notes may have been (but possibly aren't!) it is not the same as first-hand knowledge of one's own.

9. In an all age school, younger children can profit from the example of the older children—for instance, in 'family' groups at the dinner-table—if the tone of the school is good. At the same time, the presence of the younger children can help the older ones, particularly older girls. Small responsibilities for the care of the younger ones can be given to them, and at the same time practical subjects can acquire purpose and motive in the provision of necessary equipment for the lowest classes, for instance, the making of play overalls, Wendy house curtains, and tablecloths in needlework, simple toys and activity apparatus in woodwork. It is true that the same things can be made for a neighbouring school, but the urgency of the purpose is much less immediate to a subnormal child, and the project becomes more artificial.

Secondary modern schools for girls sometimes make arrangements to 'adopt' a neighbouring nursery, and the girls go in two's for a week at a time to help there, in order to overcome the isolation from young children which results from reorganisation: it is to be supposed that the Authorities which welcome and encourage such projects recognise that there are social disadvantages to be set against the scholastic advantages of reorganisation, at the same time considering that the advantages preponderate. But with subnormal children the scholastic advantages are less and the scholastic disadvantages greater, so the social disadvantages may be held to become more important.

It is fair to conclude from all this that there are sufficient relevant differences between the E.S.N. school and the ordinary school to make it unsafe to argue from one to the other and that whatever be the policy for the ordinary schools, special education is different enough to need its own policy.

On the one side there remains the perfectly valid argument that expensive equipment can most economically be provided if certain schools only, contain older children: on the other, the social and educational disadvantages of the process. A final consideration emerges at this point.

10. Reorganisation necessarily increases the catchment area, and hence the distances that children need to travel to school. Consider, for instance, the following diagram, limited for the sake of simplicity to three schools.

A, B, and C are three neighbouring mixed all-age E.S.N. schools. Although I say 'neighbouring', they are still some distance apart—a much larger distance than separates the ordinary schools of the district, because for obvious reasons they serve a much wider area. It is decided to turn A into a secondary school for boys, B into a secondary school for girls, and C into a primary mixed school. Immediately the catchment area of all three schools is widened to include the whole area formerly covered by each separately, i.e. within the dotted line. Here again the analogy with ordinary schools is faulty, because in large cities the schools are so near that under reorganisation, infant and junior and secondary schools can be provided within a relatively small compass, and travelling difficulties are few and in any case confined to the older children. Even in the first instance, each special school covered a wide area, and now the area has become much greater—and for children of all ages, note, not merely for the older ones. The cost of the additional transport thus entailed goes far to offset any saving on equipment. Furthermore, there are social and educational costs as well as monetary ones. Over-tired children, leaving home in some cases as early as 8 a.m., are in no condition to profit from the special education provided for them when they finally arrive. The hours during which the school is open must be curtailed and all the work of the school crammed into a short day to allow the buses to leave on time. Is a short day essential in the interests of the children? Yes, if they are to be over-taxed by routine grind with an over-emphasis on bookwork; but if their curriculum is well diversified and provides an adequate element of practical and aesthetic pursuits, as it should be in a good E.S.N. school, it will not tire them unduly. Again, a short day means that those children who live near the school have plenty of time on their hands and may get into mischief if they are so disposed. Clubs and after school activities are out of the question because of transport difficulties, and evening meetings for parents are similarly not easy to arrange. In fact, one sometimes gets the impression that the whole organisation of the school is geared to considerations of transport—a clear case of the tail wagging the dog. With a smaller catchment area, many of these disadvantages could be avoided, and the organisation of the school simplified.

In the last resort, a special school is not primarily a *building* which is a centre for a complicated bus schedule and in which is housed a number of pieces of elaborate and up-to-date equipment: it is a place where *children* are given special educational treatment, and their welfare must always have first consideration. While it is desirable to have as good equipment as possible, it can be purchased at too dear a price if it entails the sacrifice of more important goals: even if a somewhat higher standard of achievement in one or two directions is made possible for some of those with special abilities, that is not the final answer.

It is possible (though not necessarily desirable) for a teacher of brighter pupils, say in a technical school, to concentrate entirely on improving their skill in whatever craft they are pursuing, but such an attitude would be entirely stultifying for a teacher of subnormal children. The 'results' he gains are not likely to be of such a high standard, technically, to be regarded as sole ends in themselves, though they may very well be a useful by-product and a source of confidence and pleasure to the child. He must look for his results over a wider field and include in his purview the social and emotional as well as the intellectual development of his charges. For these reasons, the additional skill in a particular direction that may be attributable to better equipment, excellent though it is in itself, cannot outweigh the drawbacks that are inescapable if special schools are organised so that there is a break at the age of eleven.

RESIDENTIAL SCHOOLS

For various reasons, some educationally subnormal children may need to be educated away from home. In country districts, the children who need special education on account of mental handicap may be scattered over a wide area, so that travelling daily is out of the question, and it is either a residential school or nothing. In both town and country there are always likely to be some subnormal children who need to go to a boarding school because their home is a bad one, because they have no home, or because they are out of control or delinquent. All things considered, it is probably true to say that children attending residential schools are likely to have histories of especial difficulty, more so than those who attend E.S.N. day schools. There may be exceptions to this in the residential schools of rural counties, but even there difficult backgrounds are likely to preponderate. Social factors thus take on a still more urgent role than they do in day schools.

Whatever may be said against a break at eleven plus for

children who attend day schools can be urged with double force for children in boarding schools. For them the school must be their home, and for some of them, it is the only home they have. A change of school involves greater dislocation for them than it does for a day school child, because the readjustment required is total—yet these are the very children whose powers of adjustment are less even than those of the average subnormal child. It is generally agreed that children who lack a steady home background need especial help and care and the slow growth of meaningful relationships over a period of time, and how can this take place if they are gratuitously uprooted in the middle of their school life? It is a wanton threat to whatever sense of security they have managed to build. From the teacher's point of view, too, there is more and not less need to know the children than there is in a day school, and again what was said earlier on this point applies with greater force. Furthermore, the presence of a mixture of ages is more valuable in a residential school than it is to day school children who have no lack of contacts with younger and older children, if not in their family at least in those of their friends at home. The fear of undesirable practices can be overstated, if the tone of the school is good, and negative attitudes should not have the last word in the building up of policy. As I write, there keeps running in my mind a picture of three residential E.S.N. schools, each of which contains senior girls. One takes seniors only, receiving its children at the age of eleven plus from a separate school a few miles away: a second has juniors of both sexes in addition to the senior girls: the third is for girls only, but the youngest are eight or nine. There is a marked difference in the tone of these schools, much to the disadvantage of the first. Now obviously to make comparisons between the three would be full of pitfalls as there are so many factors which have not been taken into account, but at least it can be said that the experience of the second and third schools shows positively that no ill effects need follow the mixing of ages, nor even the mixing of sexes. The first school has many advantages, including an unusually good headmistress, and yet—why should the girls be as they are, shallow, uncertain, seemingly without roots? The picture to my mind is uncomfortably like that of the classic 'institution child' made familiar by the Curtis Report: and at least we can say that it has not helped them to get roots to be moved about as they have been, whether this is the whole of the story, or not. Again, it may be said that the presence of the little boys in the second school may have helped the big girls, but they themselves went elsewhere at eleven, and so had a broken history. Few authorities have been bold enough to set up a mixed residential E.S.N. school for all ages, and indeed the difficulties are formidable, but when they can be overcome the result is often very good. When all is said and done, life is co-educational, even if the schools are not. Whatever the merits of mixed schools for older children, at least there is plenty of evidence to show that older and younger children can be together to the advantage of both. Those who advocate 'family groupings' in residential schools may not carry the day yet when it comes to mixing the sexes, but it is perfectly possible to have a mixture of ages and to do away with the thoroughly undesirable practice of moving children from one school to another like so many puppets when they reach the age of eleven.

CHAPTER V

De-ascertainment

THIS cumbrous phrase[1] is used for the process which reverses that which led to a child's transfer to a special school. He is 'ascertained' as being in need of special educational treatment, and if that need is deemed to be at an end, he is said to be 'de-ascertained'. This may occur at a point during his school career, or at the end of it. Somewhat different issues are raised by these two cases, and it is as well to treat them separately.

A. *De-ascertainment during school life*

Prior to 1944, if a child was sent to a special M.D. school, it was to all intents and purposes a permanent placement. Since presumably he was sent there only because he was an 'educable mental defective' his condition could not be alleviated, however excellent the education he received. To transfer a child back to the ordinary school was tantamount to admitting that he had mistakenly been sent to the M.D. school in the first instance. Although transfers did occasionally occur they were not common (one may suspect that the mistakes were more frequent than the rectification of them). With the passing of the 1944 Act, and the substitution of 'educationally subnormal' for 'mentally deficient' the position changed considerably. The much wider connotation of educational subnormality and

---

[1] This phrase has no official standing, but is one which has crept into use. I use it here as a convenient, though ugly, shorthand expression, to avoid the repetition of more prolix descriptions.

specifically the inclusion of those who were backward in school attainments for causes *other than low intelligence,* meant that it was possible for a child to be educationally subnormal at one time and not at another. A permanent state was no longer an inherent part of the definition. It was not, therefore, impossible for a headmaster to claim that a boy had ceased to be educationally subnormal as it would formerly have been for him to claim that the boy had ceased to be mentally deficient. No admission of error on anybody's part was thereby involved, indeed it might even be considered evidence of successful effort on the part of the E.S.N. school, if a child was 'improved' and sent back to the ordinary school. A cynic might say that the new dispensation made it easier for Authorities to commit errors of judgment in the selection of children for the special school, but it also made it easier for them to rectify them without loss of face. But a principle much more important than mere face-saving is involved in all this widening of scope—the principle that a much larger number of children than the 1 or 2 per cent who would be considered mentally deficient under the old definition need special educational treatment, and that those who need it should be able to have it without being debarred by unduly rigid limits of who is 'subject to be dealt with'. Special educational treatment thus assumes a remedial aspect, and deals with children whose need is temporary as well as with those whose need is permanent.

On these premises, there may be need for teachers in E.S.N. schools to re-think their objectives and to adopt a remedial function in addition to their previous task of helping those who are permanently disabled. Then again, what *is* an 'error of judgment' in selection? Is it an error of judgment for an Authority to transfer a boy from a very large class where he has made no headway whatsoever to a small class where he can be helped, whatever his I.Q.?—indeed it can be argued that to salvage a boy of relatively good ability is a more rewarding use of time and effort and good facilities than to expend the same on one whose limitations are permanent.

Certainly there is a case for helping such boys, but the foregoing argument assumes that there are *no* facilities, other than those in the E.S.N. school, for providing special educational treatment. This assumption may all too often be correct in fact, but is it defensible in principle? We come back to the essential questions: (1) What is to happen to mentally handicapped pupils if places in the E.S.N. school are taken up by improvable cases? (2) Is the E.S.N. school the *best* place for giving remedial help?

The 1944 Act has now been in operation long enough for a body of experience to be available regarding the way in which these new problems and opportunities are working out in practice in E.S.N. schools, and for tentative observations to be made on the trends which appear to be developing as a result.

It is not easy for teachers in E.S.N. schools always to remember that they may now be catering for two groups of children whose needs are very different, their permanent clientèle and abler individuals who are nevertheless very backward. Things go on much as they have always gone on, and the whole tone and tempo is undemanding: no need to fear that expectations of improvement are set too high. But the occasional brighter child may merge only too successfully into the general background.

For instance, Evelyn came to England at the age of ten when her mother's marriage to an American had finally broken up. For various reasons, she had received very little schooling until she entered an English junior school, still a complete non-reader. Perhaps if her native language had been other than English, the examiner would have been more ready to distinguish between lack of reading and lack of capacity to read: as it was, she was promptly sent to the E.S.N. school, in spite

of an I.Q. of 88. She had plenty to say for herself and her con-
versation and width of general information made her stand
out from the rest of the children there in a way which one
would have thought could not be missed, except that it *was*
missed. She was transferred with the rest at the age of eleven
to a secondary E.S.N. school, and neither school seemed to consider her needs as in any way different from those of other
children. She has adapted herself only too well to her surroundings and as she is now nearly thirteen it seems unlikely that
she will return to the ordinary school. She is progressing—at
the special school pace, though not at her own—and her attitude to learning is compliant, that is, she responds to any help
and encouragement she receives but is not *so* enthusiastic that
in its absence she will carry on and go ahead on her own. This
seems to be a case of getting the worst of both worlds, for had
she remained in the ordinary school she would, being the girl
she is, probably have responded to the higher expectations the
teachers held for her. In fairness to the special school, it must
be said that no suggestion that Evelyn was rather different from
the others was made by the Authority at the time of the placement. Nevertheless, it remains true that she is not receiving
the special educational treatment which she needs. It may be
said, in view of the history, that there is a possibility of emotional difficulties, but if this is so, she still is not getting the
appropriate help.

Other teachers and schools are more aware of the possibility
of returning children to the ordinary school. In one or two
instances, it may even seem as if the policy of the school is
being considerably if not unduly influenced by this possibility.
This is a case where the proof of the pudding is in the eating
and one can but wait and see what trends develop and how the
possibility of de-ascertainment is actually affecting the work of
the E.S.N. schools. Straws in the wind are not entirely reassuring. Talk of 'scholarships' (when a child is de-ascertained and

returned to the ordinary school) is no doubt partly a joke, but it can easily become more than a joke and lead to undesirable competition between schools. It is said that there are already schools which make a boast of the number of their children who return to the ordinary school. It is a short step from this to set out, of deliberate policy, to increase that number, and if this happens the door is open to several undesirable consequences, in the way of cramming some and neglecting and depreciating others. Every good teacher likes to see some result for his labours, in which he can take pride. When he enters an E.S.N. school, a teacher must forgo the most obvious forms of gratification, and gain his results over a wider area than scholastic attainment. There is danger of a covert reintroduction of scholastic goals underneath a drive for de-ascertainment, and a corresponding depreciation of those who are unable to reach the standard involved. I myself think that this implicit depreciation is more damaging to a child's self-respect than any actual neglect which may be involved.

There seems to be need for a middle way, between never returning children to the ordinary school, and making this the focus of attention; and the key is to be found in differentiating between the needs of different children. The justification of special school education is not to be found in making it one more kind of forcing-house like the rest, but at a lower level, nor in giving up all attempt at instruction, even in cases where it is appropriate, but in allowing each child to progress at his own pace. This may result in certain children returning to the ordinary school, and this is creditable, but it is no more creditable than the efforts of a less-endowed child to develop at his own level. The teacher can take pride in both.

We may conclude that the de-ascertainment of certain children is a dangerous goal of endeavour for the E.S.N. school to set itself, but it may be an occasional by-product.

The amount of de-ascertainment that goes on is likely to

depend less on the school than on the Local Authority, as it is largely a function of the latter's admission policy. The calibre of the children will in the long run determine whether there is much or little 'improvement' to be expected from them, and this is a further argument against the unwisdom of setting up the number of those sent back to the ordinary school as a test of the efficiency of a school. Two E.S.N. schools in different areas where the policy of the Authority is different may be equally efficient and yet have quite different de-ascertainment records: it would be as foolish to compare them as it would be to compare the number of grammar school places in a junior school in a slum area and in a comfortable district.

The final questions that must be considered are the questions of policy raised earlier, whether in fact the E.S.N. school is the *best* place in which remedial help can be given, and if so, how priorities are to be established between the claims of different groups on places in the E.S.N. school.

The advantages of E.S.N. schools can be summarised as— smaller classes than in ordinary schools, individual work, and less rigid organisation. As against these advantages, the E.S.N. school as a place for remedial work suffers from a number of disadvantages.

1. As we have seen, it is not always easy for teachers to keep a balance between the claims of the innately handicapped and the claims of remedial work. One or other is likely to suffer.

2. It greatly increases the problems of organisation of the E.S.N. school if the range of Mental Age is considerably increased. (This point was dealt with in Chapter III.)

3. Occasional returns of a few children to the ordinary school are one thing; but if it is a set *policy* to admit many children whose need for special educational treatment is transitory, their passage can be disturbing to those who must of necessity always remain, even if the teachers are careful to avoid partiality. Discouragement cannot always be avoided in

this event, both to the children and to their parents, and the latter may be less careful than the teachers and express their disapproval openly to their children.

4. The transfer of children to an E.S.N. school is rather a cumbrous procedure hedged about with safeguards and appeals and examinations. It is true that the process of certification has now been abolished (except where there are irreconcilable disputes) but even so it is quite a time-consuming business to get a child into a special school, and having got him in, to get him out again.

5. This leads to a question of parents' attitudes, for the E.S.N. school as a place for remedial work is likely to be handicapped by parental suspicion. Prejudice against the former 'silly school' dies hard, and that offensive epithet is still to be heard, and is not reassuring. Where a boy needs to attend an E.S.N. school for the rest of his school life this opposition has to be faced and can be overcome, but it seems rather gratuitous to brave it if a shortish period of help is all that is envisaged. It may be that the Authority is hoping to use this 'remedial' function as itself a weapon to break down parental distrust, if it becomes generally known that children do in fact return to the ordinary school. But that takes a long time, and in any case is likely to prove a boomerang if it disturbs the parents of 'permanent' children. One Authority, starting an E.S.N. school for the first time, and anxious for it to be successful, was rash enough to assure parents that *all* the children from it would improve sufficiently to return to the ordinary school: the difficulties which it thus made for itself can easily be imagined.

6. Under no conceivable circumstances is it likely that an Authority would use its E.S.N. schools for *all* its remedial work, and additional arrangements would still need to be made elsewhere. *Bright* non-readers, though technically educationally subnormal, are unlikely to be sent, and in practice the children

would be those who were fairly dull, though above the level of mental handicap, and improvable in that limited sense only. I have used the word 'remedial' as a convenient shorthand expression in this chapter, but in a narrower sense than its usual meaning. The disadvantage, it seems to me, of using the E.S.N. school for *some* of its improvable children is that it duplicates work which will have to be done outside in any case, and suggests, misleadingly, that the whole field of special educational treatment is being covered when only a portion of it is really. Remedial work with bright children remains outside its ken, and so does the greater part of catering for the very dull—a brief consideration of the numbers involved proves that, as was pointed out in the section on ascertainment.

7. Finally, any use of special school places for improvable children can only cut down the numbers of the permanently handicapped whom it can accommodate.

We may conclude, then, that it would be an unwise policy for an Authority to set out to develop the remedial function of its E.S.N. school, since such development could only be at the expense of its 'permanent' clients, and also since the E.S.N. school suffers from a number of drawbacks which make it not the best place in which such remedial help can be given. I would suggest that the strongest claim on places in E.S.N. schools remains with those children whose innate handicap is the greatest, so that they are likely to need to stay in the special school all their school life. De-ascertainment, therefore, should not become a major aim of the policy of schools or Authorities, though it should be readily available for a minority of children.

B. *School Leavers*

The transition from school to work is a milestone in any child's life: for one who is leaving an E.S.N. school it is doubly important, because he may be able to be merged within the everyday world, or he may prove to be incapable of independent adult adjustment.

The continuing emphasis, undoubtedly, of employers and neighbours will be on social, not intellectual or educational, adequacy. They will not mind what his intelligence quotient is, nor how well he can read and calculate, but the criterion that is adopted is the practical one of the individual's capacity to lead a normal life without special help. If his limitations of mind and character are such that he cannot do that, then he is subnormal and will need help.

This criterion differs considerably from those which are adopted when considering whether a child should be classed as educationally subnormal. Even in the old days, when 'mental defect' had to be established before a boy or girl could be admitted to an M.D. school, there were differences of emphasis between the definitions of 'defect' under the Education Acts and under the Mental Deficiency Acts. These differences can be summed up by saying that the emphasis of the former was on intellectual failure, and on the need for special education, and of the latter on failure in social adjustment. Their territories, while roughly the same, had different boundaries, and it might happen that only one applied. For instance, a steady stolid hardworking boy who had rightly been sent to the M.D. school on account of his limited ability might nevertheless be able to earn his living in adult life, marry and bring up a family and keep out of trouble, so that he could not be considered 'mentally defective' in the social sense of the Mental Deficiency Acts. Another boy of unstable temperament, who though very dull had a higher I.Q. than the first and thus never needed to attend a special M.D. school, might be a constant anxiety to everyone on account of his irresponsibility, and so socially incompetent that (having come before the courts and so become subject to be dealt with) he needed to be certified in adult life as mentally defective.

Hence, even before the passing of the 1944 Act, there was

need for a reassessment of special school boys and girls at school-leaving age in order to determine whether or not they came within the scope of the M.D. Acts. It is important to note that no contradiction was involved, whatever the decision reached, as the same person could be certifiable as a child for educational purposes, and yet not a defective within the meaning of the Mental Deficiency Acts. De-certification on leaving the special school at the age of sixteen could be, and was, practised prior to 1944: thus the passage of the 1944 Education Act made a greater difference in respect of de-ascertainment during school life than it did in respect of de-ascertainment at sixteen.

The position from 1944 to 1959 was as follows. In theory, the Mental Deficiency Acts covered the whole life-span of the defective from birth to death, but their operation was waived in the case of *educable* children until the end of their school life, during which time the children came within the scope of the Education Act. Special educational treatment under the Education Act could have been given from the age of 2 onwards and could continue until the age of sixteen, or even beyond: it need not, necessarily, have been given in a special school, but could have been given by approved arrangements in an ordinary school. While this treatment was in operation, the Mental Deficiency Acts were, so to speak, suspended, and a decision as to whether the child came within the scope of the Mental Deficiency Acts was held in abeyance until he came to leave school. Another way of putting this would be to say that he was given every chance to show that he was *not* defective by his response to the special opportunities that he had had.

A final statutory examination held before he left school determined whether he was to be 'reported' to the Mental Deficiency Committee as a defective, or whether he was to be de-ascertained and go out into the world as an independent citizen like any other. At that examination a large number of factors were taken into account: the young person's health, physique, and temperament, his emotional stability and self-control, his ability to settle down and work steadily, his adjustment to other people, both those of his own age and those in authority, his suggestibility, his acceptance of setbacks and so on. His school record would show whether he had made progress over the years, not only in school work, but also in learning to govern his impulses and to get on with others: he might or might not have been in trouble with the police: and there might have been reports from clinics, Care Committees, etc., which had a bearing on the matter. Above all, there were the circumstances of his home to be considered—whether he was amenable to the influence of his parents, whether that influence was likely to be used wisely, the presence of particularly favourable or unfavourable factors, etc.

If it was felt that the outlook for his future was good, if he was a steady though limited youth from a good home, of whom the school spoke well, he might have been de-ascertained. It should be noted, however, that de-ascertainment was a grave step to take in that it was removing the boy from all outside supervision, and if there was any doubt in the matter it was probably safer to report him. Supervision under the Mental Deficiency Acts need not have been rigorous, but their support was then available in case of need.

The position changed again in 1959, with the passage of the Mental Health Act, which superseded the former Mental Deficiency Acts. Section 57 of the Education Act has in consequence been repealed and replaced by the Second Schedule of the Mental Health Act. The main changes affecting this book are:

1. Terminology. The old categories of the Mental Deficiency Acts are replaced by 'subnormal', 'severely subnormal', and 'psychopathic'.

2. Parents can ask repeatedly for decisions to be reviewed (e.g. if they do not agree that their child is unsuitable for school) and they have extended rights of appeal. The ascertainment of a severely subnormal child is thus less final than it used to be.

3. Provisions for training such children are now mandatory on Local Authorities, and not merely permissive. Attendance at day Training Centres (formerly Occupation Centres) can be compelled.

4. The notion of 'inexpediency' has been repealed, though temporary exclusion of troublesome children can still occur.

5. Statutory supervision is replaced by voluntary supervision: if it is not accepted nothing can be done then. A seriously deviant or criminal person *might* later become the subject of an order, but in general compulsion is eschewed.

6. The formal procedure of 'notification' is replaced by a 'decision', which must be recorded and copies given to the Local Authority and the parent. Local Education Authorities can still pass on information to the Mental Health Committee and it is desirable that they should, but it is no longer essential that this should be done while the child is of school age.

The first points will be considered in the next chapter: here, where our concern is with school leavers, it is the last two that need discussion.

These two changes together take away from the *crucial* importance of the examination at school-leaving age, though it remains a valuable opportunity for reviewing the child's assets and handicaps and for considering how best he can be helped, as a person, in employment, and in his spare time. Some Heads of special schools regret the disappearance of statutory supervision: they say that it is the unstable subnormal child from the rather better home whose parents, realising his weaknesses, agree to voluntary supervision, while a similar child from a really unsatisfactory home (whose need is greater still) is liable to get no help because co-operation is not forthcoming. Prevention, they say, is better than cure: by the time the young person becomes the subject of an order under the Act, much harm has been done that might have been avoided. As against this, others hold that coercion got super-vision off to a wrong start and that it is more realistic to recog-nise that little of value can be achieved without co-operation, so that it is better to limit the element of compulsion to cases where incapacity to adjust to society is *proved* and not a matter of opinion. Naturally, all Heads will hope that matters will not come to this, and that many children who come up for review will have stabilised sufficiently not to need to be reported.

Up to a point, then, it can be said that integration within the general community at school-leaving age provides a suitable goal towards which the E.S.N. school can orient itself, in a way which returning children to ordinary schools does not. The emphasis in the school-leaving examination, as we have seen, is on all-round development; school attainments are taken into account, but the main weight is placed on steadi-ness and reliability, on good habits and conduct, on social adjustment. Teachers in E.S.N. schools can take pride in the achievement by their pupils of confidence and maturity and in their willingness to accept their own limitations. At the same time, there are many factors involved which are entirely out of the control of the school and which may be decisive in deter-mining a child's future, and it would be unrealistic of the teachers to set their expectations for the children too high, to the extent that they are disappointed if, in spite of all their efforts, the children have to be reported. If certain children are able to be de-ascertained, that is very good, but if others have to be reported, it does not mean that the school has failed them.

It cannot be too strongly emphasised that reporting is not punitive in intention, but is meant for the *protection* of the individual and of society. It would be quite wrong for that protection to be withheld, when the whole circumstances are unfavourable. I have met teachers who felt that they should press for de-ascertainment and considered it as a reflection on their competence if de-ascertainment was not granted, but that is surely misguided. If the limitations of the young persons are such that they *cannot* stand alone and make an independent social adjustment, it is unrealistic to refuse to accept this fact and the consequences which it entails.

Perhaps, rather than say that de-ascertainment is a legitimate goal, it would be clearer to say that the school aims to foster the all-round development of its pupils. In specially favourable circumstances, the development may be enough to result in de-ascertainment.

Finally, I add some comments on the practice whereby some children are reassessed and allowed to leave the E.S.N. school at the age of fifteen instead of at the special school-leaving age of sixteen, a practice which is not quite the same as either of the main types of de-ascertainment that have been discussed.

Suppose a senior boy or girl is making particularly good progress at the E.S.N. school, to the extent that there is talk of returning him to the ordinary school (Type A). If he is twelve or thirteen, that may well be done, and should be done without delay, but if he is fourteen or over the difficulty arises that it is hardly worth while in view of the short time before he would leave the modern school on attaining the age of fifteen. Instead, he is retained in the E.S.N. school, the statutory examination at school leaving is put forward a year, he is de-ascertained (Type B) as soon as he is fifteen, and he is then free to leave and go to work at once, as he is over the usual school-leaving age.

It is a practice which is very popular with the young persons concerned and with their parents, for obvious reasons, but it does raise some rather awkward doubts as to its long-term effects if the practice were to become at all general.

1. The possibility of being allowed to leave school early is said to provide a most salutary incentive to effort. No doubt it does, among those who are likely to be released, but its effect on the remainder is more doubtful. Low-grade children, and those whose homes are particularly bad, are almost bound to be reported at sixteen however hard they may try. I can think of no better way of instilling discontent and discouragement into the majority, for conscious effort is only one of the factors involved and the others are out of the boy's control altogether. In the short run it may seem stimulating, but it is likely to boomerang.

2. Parents are encouraged to 'try on' demands and hard luck stories, and may be a considerable nuisance both to the school and to the Authority. More serious, if an exception cannot be made for their boy, they may blame and even punish him in their annoyance. If the school, which should know better, allows it to be thought that sufficient effort will lead to the release of the boy, parents cannot be expected to distinguish between lack of effort and lack of ability.

3. To some extent this problem is a result of sending children to the E.S.N. school at too late an age. If children entered the E.S.N. school earlier, they might be improved in time to return to the ordinary school (De-ascertainment Type A) and the whole difficulty could be avoided. Furthermore, it is bound to raise the question, if these children are so easily and so completely improved, whether they should ever have been admitted to the school in the first place?

4. It has for many years been a cardinal principle of policy that children whose difficulties are such that they need to go to an E.S.N. school require a longer period of training than the average child. When the school-leaving age was fourteen the age of leaving from the E.S.N. school was 16—a difference of

two years—as compared with the present gap of only one year. This longer period of training should be thought of positively as an opportunity for giving effective help. Too many parents still conceive of it negatively, as a sort of punishment. For schools, by short-sighted acts, to connive at reinforcing this impression, is indeed to cut the ground from under their own feet, when they come to explain to parents the meaning of the training they are trying to give and the reason why the leaving age of the special school is higher than the normal. It may be that a few children have rightly been released at the age of fifteen—are they children who ever should have entered, one wonders?—but the disservice to the ideals and aims of special school education is tremendous.

5. It was suggested earlier that, where doubt existed, it was safer to report than to de-ascertain, i.e. even at the age of sixteen, the decision to de-ascertain a child who, after all, is considerably handicapped, is a grave one and should only be made when the examining doctor is satisfied that it can be made without risk. A year earlier, in the middle of adolescence, there is bound to be less evidence available and correspondingly greater risk in sending a boy or girl into the adult world.

I would suggest that, so far from being evidence of unusual success, it is evidence of *failure* if children are sent from special schools before reaching the age of sixteen—failure on the part of those responsible for selection, for if the children can truly be sent into the world at fifteen, their case cannot have been very serious and their place could have been taken by others whom more careful search would have discovered; and also failure on the part of the schools to realise the measure of their opportunities and responsibilities to deeply handicapped children, and to see the unwelcome repercussions of superficially attractive expedients on the long-term attitudes of parents and others to the training which the special school provides.

CHAPTER VI

Seriously Handicapped Children

RECENT years have seen a great increase of interest in, and provision for, the severely subnormal. Voluntary bodies such as the National Association for Mental Health and the National Society for Mentally Handicapped Children have for long been campaigning for better facilities for children who are at present outside the scope of the education services, and the impact of their work on public opinion is increasing. Both nationally and locally, there are demands for more to be done. Researches, such as those of the Clarkes at Epsom, and Tizard and his colleagues in the Brooklands experiment, are tending to produce a more optimistic estimate of the potentialities of the severely handicapped than was formerly held: there is less emphasis on inherent limitation, and more on environmental stimulation and favourable response to training. Medical advances raise hopes for the future, as for instance in the control of phenylketonuria or the causation of mongolism. At a time of full employment, experiments in training adult subnormals were widely reported as encouraging hopes of employability greater than had previously been entertained. Some of these hopes may prove illusory, a general recession may cruelly limit possibilities of employment, but the general awakening of public concern cannot be gainsaid. It is perhaps significant of a more positive approach that in the title of the new Act of 1959 the words 'Mental Health' have replaced 'Mental Deficiency'. It is certainly significant that provisions for training severely subnormal children are now enjoined as a *duty* on local authorities. This is a reform of the greatest importance, since it has led directly to the enormous expansion of facilities that has occurred in the last few years and is still continuing. This is not only a matter of bricks and mortar (though the appearance of handsome and purpose-built new buildings is a welcome sign of increased public interest in the welfare of the handicapped) but, more importantly, the recruitment and training of staff to work with the children. Not only are more workers needed, but an attempt is being made to raise the prestige of this exacting work by introducing courses of study and training, with recognised qualifications at the end. It is not suggested that the devoted commitment of those who worked in the old Occupation Centres during the last forty years has been superseded (no paper qualifications can replace insight and devotion), but on the contrary, that it is at last gaining recognition. The change of title from Occupation to Training Centres is symptomatic of a positive widening of function, a challenge to the skill of those who work in these Centres.

Let us now trace the various ways and stages at which children enter these Centres. Some come under the purview of the Mental Health Committee in babyhood (these are likely to be extremely subnormal children whose handicap is obvious) and others are discovered by clinics, health visitors, etc., during the pre-school years. At the age of five compulsory school attendance brings a further number of children to the notice of School Medical Officers. Some of these are clearly severely handicapped and (if the parents do not dispute the decision) are referred to the Mental Health Authority. Others are borderline cases who might respond to special education, and then again might not. When any doubt exists, the child must be given the benefit of it and such children are retained within the school system and their progress noted, until it is possible to come to a clear-cut decision about them. Even if they prove

68

to be educable, it is almost certain (unless the first impression was badly mistaken) that they will need to go to a special school. As time passes, it becomes clear which children are responding in school, and which are not. Although no limit is laid down and children can be, and are, reported as unsuitable for education at school at any point in their school life, there is much to be said in favour of an early decision, say not later than seven or eight. Once it is quite clear that a child cannot remain in any school with profit, it is far better, for everybody's sake, for the change to be made than for it to be postponed. It is harder for parents to accept the decision the longer it is delayed, and it is not fair to the child to keep him in a situation that is quite beyond him and by the same token to keep him away from the training which he requires. Those in charge of Training Centres are anxious to receive children as soon as possible in order that they can start early on a training which is at their level, and from which they can profit. At the same time, the teachers in E.S.N. schools are freed from their presence and are able to give fuller attention to the children who can profit, the genuinely educationally subnormal children.

A severely subnormal child who is allowed to remain in the special school is not only failing to profit himself, but he is occupying a place which another child needs. Difficulties follow in ever-widening circles: the parents of genuinely educationally subnormal children are reluctant to send them to the special school, although it is in their best interests: teachers in the ordinary school are tempted to agree with them, and children are retained in the ordinary school who should be in the special school, to the detriment alike of themselves, their teachers and the rest of the class. E.S.N. school teachers, who criticise the teachers in the ordinary school for hanging on to the children much too long, may reflect that that is exactly what they are doing themselves if they neglect their *duty* to call for review of children who are not profiting. The only ways to cut through the vicious circle is for all children who are known to be ineducable to be excluded, for however amenable they may be, that is not the point. After all, a special school is a *school*, it is not a Training Centre, and it cannot help the children as much as the Training Centre could.

It is my impression that this is one respect in which there has been real progress within the last few years and that E.S.N. schools are indeed improving their standard. Recently, I had occasion to visit a special school which I had known well ten years previously and was very struck by the difference. Formerly it contained many low-grade children, and its reputation was low, so that it was difficult to induce parents and teachers to agree to the transfer of a child there: there was no Training Centre in the district, a thickly populated one, and therefore it was difficult to have children excluded, however low grade they might be, for the argument always was that there was no alternative placement. Now there is a Training Centre, the severely subnormal children have been transferred, and the E.S.N. school is vastly improved—it really is in a position to give 'special education' as it should. There are, of course, other reasons for the difference, but the main one is that it is now catering for the right sort of child.

Yet even so, the improvement is far from universal and there are still schools which are unduly ready to tolerate the presence of low-grade children for long periods, and Medical Officers who are unduly slow to decide that they should be reported to the Mental Health Committee, although all reasonable doubt is at an end.

The decision to remove a child from school is a grave one to take, but once it is evident that it is the right one, delay can do no good. The so-called 'trial period' in an E.S.N. school is open to some criticism on this score, at least as it is working out in practice. Children of pre-school age are, and always have been, reported without delay if their condition warrants it, and the same holds good for five- and six-year-olds if they are clearly unsuitable for school. It is not necessary that they should all first pass through an E.S.N. school, but in some cases this interpretation is being put upon the Ministry's recommendation of a trial period (which is, of course, essential where genuine doubt exists). Where it does not, the delay can only confuse and mislead the parents. It must be remembered that the distinction between 'educationally subnormal' and 'severely subnormal' is not easily conveyed to most ordinary people, and that there is no merit in simply substituting two terrible blows for one. They are not felt less on that account, but rather more, and it is better to face the issue squarely in the first place than to seek to postpone it, by what is sometimes felt by the parent (however unjustly) to be verbal quibbles, and resented as such.

A number of people consider that the present position in England and Wales, whereby severely subnormal children pass from the purview of the Education Authority to that of the Mental Health Committee, cannot be defended, and would prefer a situation where the Education Authorities retain the responsibility for such children, as in Scotland. A Training Centre, they argue, is in its own way an educational establishment: it is wrong to make a sharp distinction between education (given in schools) and training (given in Training Centres): and it is illogical to draw a hard and fast line at a particular point since the variation in intelligence is admitted to be continuous and therefore the children just below the line differ very little from those above it, yet they are treated very differently. The defenders of the *status quo* reply that, if children are ineducable, then by definition the Education Authorities are the wrong ones to be dealing with them. The counter reply is likely to be that the Ministry of Education should rightly think of itself as the Ministry for Children—all children, including the

71

deeply handicapped. From this point, the argument branches out over wide areas—Parliament did not take that view when entrusting the central responsibility for the new Children's Committees to the Home Office and not to either the Education or Health Ministries, and so on—and it is unnecessary to follow it further once it has become lost in the mazes of high policy.

I would like to make two comments on the logic of the matter.

1. The claim that switching over from one department to another is foolish seems a strong one, until we remember that it must take place somewhere. There is no question that, at the lowest end, looking after idiots who are entirely confined to bed is a matter for hospitals and nursing care, i.e. is a medical question. Similarly, there is no question that at the upper end, the provision of grammar school places is an educational matter, and not the concern of doctors. Somewhere in between is a no-man's land which is claimed in turn by the medical and by the educational auxiliaries—for instance, some say that selection of children for E.S.N. schools should be in the hands of psychologists, as it is an educational matter, others that it comes undoubtedly within the province of the doctor, and so on. If a belt is twisted and fastened, then whether the turnover comes at one end or another or in the middle is arguable, but turnover there must be somewhere. The issue then resolves itself into finding the best place for the change.

2. It is fallacious to argue that where there is continuous variation it is impossible to make any sort of differentiation at all. Where does 'little' cease to be little and become 'big'? Obviously the choice of *any* change-point can be pilloried, yet there is sense in calling some objects, like the Eiffel Tower, big, and others, like ants, little. As Stebbing said,[1] 'Failure to recognise that it is not logically possible to draw a sharp line between those who possess and those who do not possess a property

[1] *Thinking to Some Purpose*, p. 181.

72

capable of being present in any one of a continuous series of intermediate degrees leads us into making either of two serious logical blunders. On the one hand, we may deny that there is any difference between the extremes because they are thus connected. On the other hand, we may illegitimately demand that a sharp line should be drawn.' For administrative purposes, it may be necessary to define limits or boundaries. *Wherever* the boundary is made it will be a target for criticism, but that does not mean that it should be made nowhere.

These comments do not deal with the *merits* of the case, but only with the *logical* issues involved. I have found that arguments of the form 'You can't draw a line here or here or here, so you can't do it anywhere' are often spuriously convincing in appearance. The real question is where the balance of advantage lies, in helping these children. *Is* this the point at which the educationists should finally hand over to the health authorities, as they must, sooner or later? Is it merely a quibble to say that, if a child is unsuitable for school, that is the point at which the Education Authority steps out? Whatever the answer to this, there is certainly a very good case for the extension of social services catering for the deeply handicapped child, and giving advice and assistance to his parents in bearing their heavy burden. A wider provision of Training Centres in districts where they are practicable; and elsewhere, increased use of peripatetic advisers who can instruct the children in simple activities and crafts which are within their capacity, and also make suggestions about the management and training of the children, are strongly to be advocated.

Up to this point, I have been dealing only with children who are considered unsuitable for education at school because of severe subnormality. It is, however, possible for some to be considered unsuitable and excluded because of behaviour problems. This raises quite a different set of issues which can best be approached by a short digression.

Anyone who has had much experience of administration can think of occasions when the spirit of the law was best served by a little latitude in the interpretation of the letter. An unduly rigid adherence to formulae can in exceptional cases result in hardship and injustice. It is true that 'hard cases make bad laws' and that, however liberally administration proceeds, there must still be *some* limits which have to be observed; to give an entirely free hand for individuals to interpret the regulations as they pleased would be to ask for trouble. Yet at the same time not even the most omniscient human being could lay down in advance precisely *every* situation that may arise in the application of a particular regulation, and it may in practice be most helpful to have a sort of 'escape clause' which can be invoked in case of need. The essence of its usefulness lies in its deliberate vagueness—and for that very reason it has to be carefully scrutinised and used most sparingly, if it is to escape abuse.

The interpretation of the word 'unsuitable' may be such an escape clause. In certain circumstances, it may be essential for authorities to possess the power to exclude a child when the actual *evidence* would be insufficient to allow them to say he was severely subnormal, or even when the evidence suggests that he is not. Such emergencies are easier to recognise when they occur than to describe in convincing terms. For instance, Kenneth, a five-year-old boy from an excellent home, was excluded from school as being too dangerous to retain, but the evidence? Really rather thin, *unless you knew him*. To say his behaviour was incalculable gets nowhere: his intelligence quotient was unknown: it seemed impossible to establish contact with him. In short, he was uncanny, and actually no one who met him could fail to realise this. What was he? subnormal? autistic? or pre-psychotic? Whatever the answer, it was clearly to the interests of other children that he should be away from them.

But exclusion is one thing: making it permanent is quite

another. It is the difference between a short-term expedient and a long-term solution. To refer a child to the Mental Health Committee suggests that the answer to the problem he poses is known (as, of course, is the case in the ordinary situation when a doctor reports a mongol, say, as unsuitable for education at school), but this was far from being so in the example under discussion. He was learning nothing in his infant school and was aggressive with other children: but this after all is by no means unheard of in children who later settle down. The list of actual attacks on his classmates was not in itself serious and could easily have been paralleled in the record of other children whom no one would have considered excluding. His home background was comfortable: his parents were above average intelligence and his two elder sisters were doing well in the grammar school: the boy himself was handsome and upstanding. It is true that all these can be consistent with a diagnosis of severe subnormality, but they do nothing to suggest it. In such circumstances, where the answer was so evidently 'not proven', it was the plain duty of the Authority to make further investigations, and it would have been a dereliction of its responsibility had it too hastily proceeded to report him and thus closed the matter. Psychiatric diagnoses varied between 'probably imbecile', a 'rare case of very early schizophrenia', 'behaviour problem following (undiagnosed)? encephalitis in infancy'; and various expedients were tried to help him including play therapy at the local Child Guidance Clinic, and a period of in-patient treatment at the Maudsley Hospital. As he grew older it was feared that whatever his original endowment—the evidence of performance tests on the rare (and brief) occasions when he would co-operate suggested that his I.Q. might be anything from 70 upwards—he would become subnormal by deprivation if he was left without education. It must be remembered that his home circumstances were good and toys and materials were amply available at home, and for the infant school years they sufficed, but this would not always be the case. He was tried for an hour or two each day at a private school, until after some months it would no longer keep him, and then at an E.S.N. school for afternoons only. Eventually it was decided that there was no alternative to reporting him, since whatever the problem, it was not yielding to any known treatment; but at least the Authority, with the co-operation of the parents, had done everything that could be done.

Now obviously this is an exceptional case, but my point is just that the 'escape clause' should be confined to exceptional cases, and should not be used without full examination of all the possible alternatives. It is tempting for the Head Teacher of an E.S.N. or an Infant school, faced with a violent and dangerous child, to call for his exclusion. By all means, let him be excluded: but that exclusion should set in motion a really careful investigation as to *why* he behaves as he does· In many cases, perhaps the majority, reasons can generally be discovered, and the appropriate treatment (physical, or psychological, or merely removal from home, or—dare one say it?—from that particular school) put into effect with good results. (From this point of view the particular example I have given may not be a good one, if it suggests that no improvement can result and that the mystery must always remain a mystery.)

Cases have been known, unfortunately, where nothing like this careful scrutiny has been given. The story of Raymond would not seem to be possible except that it has in fact happened. Raymond was rough and boisterous, disturbed other children in his infant school by unintelligible, loud shouting, and took no notice whatever of commands or reproofs. He was excluded, reported as unsuitable for education at school, and sent to the Training Centre—all this before he was six. After he had been there for a year, representations were made by the superintendent to the authorities that the boy seemed to have more ability than the other children, and eventually at the age of seven he was sent on trial to an E.S.N. school: again his ability stood out as being superior to that of the others. Now Raymond is in fact deaf: not so deaf that (with his at least average ability) he was unable to talk when he entered school at five (had he been completely silent no doubt that obvious possibility would have been investigated), but deaf enough to make him ignore commands.

One particularly serious aspect of all this is that, once the boy has been reported, he has acquired a label and his case is considered closed—until special circumstances re-opened it. The Head Teacher, receiving a boy with such a history, was understandably apprehensive, and this apprehension was shared by the officials, who appeared incredulous when, on ringing up to enquire how Raymond was faring, they received the answer that he could continue in school—for was he not known by his papers to be violent and had he not been reported as harmful?

It is evident from this example that the escape clause should only be used with great care. Pamphlet 5 says: 'If it is impossible to correct his behaviour or habits by the usual methods of school discipline or by medical or psychological treatment, it is clearly advisable to prevent his continued attendance'[1]— obviously implying that appropriate enquiries and treatment have first been given. It is worth remembering that 'uncontrolled' (in a given situation) does not mean the same as 'uncontrollable' (in *any* situation): and Head Teachers who ask too freely for children to be excluded may simply be saying that they are themselves unable to manage recalcitrant children. From the child's point of view, he is probably better off in school than he is wandering loose, and the best chance of reclaiming him is to keep him in school, if it is at all possible. Nevertheless, the Head Teacher of an infants' or an E.S.N. school is rightly able to call upon the Authority to exclude

[1] *Op. cit.* p. 20.

children where circumstances warrant it, and should be able to rely on their unhesitating support. The moral of this example is not that the Authority should be slow to comply with the Head Teacher's request (for after all, she *is* where the shoe pinches, and her opinion must be allowed to count), but that, having excluded, they should pause and consider before reporting a child under the Mental Health Act. In any case, Authorities have power to provide education otherwise than at school for children who can benefit by it but are unable to attend school, and this should be remembered for children like Raymond.

The decision that a child is unsuitable for education at school can be made at any time during his school life, and there is more justification for a late decision on the ground of seriously deviant behaviour than on mental incapacity. Deteriorating conditions, often with an organic basis (e.g. epilepsy); gross adolescent instability; psychotic or neurotic states supervening on the original mental handicap—these are some of the reasons which may involve invoking the Mental Health Act in the middle and later years of childhood. Nearly all such children are already in the E.S.N. schools, and there is likely to be much less doubt about their condition than in the case of young children previously discussed.

Finally, at school-leaving age, as we saw in the previous chapter, the Education Authority has to reach a decision whether children who are *educationally* subnormal are also 'subnormal' in the terms of the Mental Health Act, or not. All leavers from E.S.N. schools must be examined: and in addition, registered mentally handicapped pupils who have been receiving special educational treatment in ordinary schools may be brought forward for examination. The permissive powers in respect of the latter group of children are at present not very widely known, though potentially they are of great importance, and they represent a signal departure from the position prior to 1944. Teachers of such handicapped children can play a big part in ensuring that they are not overlooked, provided they are enlightened enough to realise that in so doing they are ensuring necessary support and protection for a child who cannot stand alone, and have got beyond the silly attitude that notification is a stigma to be avoided.

Notification means in effect that the young person can be dealt with under the Mental Health Act in the way which is most appropriate to his needs. The great majority of subnormal persons are under supervision: this simply means that they remain in their ordinary surroundings at home, go to work (as many of them are able to), and receive periodical visits from the Local Authority's officers. The ordinary services that the district provides are, of course, open to them as to any other school leaver, but the difficulty is that, whereas the average young person can be left to make his own use of these services, a mentally handicapped one needs help and encouragement. This applies particularly to dwellers in large cities where the complexity of organisation is utterly baffling to many ordinary people, and certainly to all handicapped ones: they need to be given detailed help where to go, how to set about finding the appropriate service, and so on. Without this help they can so easily slip out of the ken of, for example, the Youth Employment Service, and yet they are in particular need of guidance when moving from one job to another. Tactful advice can also be given to them and their parents, for instance, on the wise outlay of money, use of leisure, choice of companions and so on. The task of the officer is to establish a friendly relationship with the young person and his family, and without being interfering, to give such guidance as can prevent more serious difficulties from arising.

Other young people are unlikely to respond to supervision, either because of their own instability or because their home conditions are particularly bad. In their own interests and for

the protection of the community they need a different placement. They may be placed under paid guardianship, while still
remaining in the open community; or they may need to be
under order. With all the developments in Community Care
that there have been since 1959, some still need to be in
sheltered communities, hospitals and institutions. In the latter
event, their case must by statute be periodically reviewed,
and if their circumstances improve (for instance, if they
themselves become more stable or if their family is better able
to have them at home) they may be released on licence, and if
that trial period proves satisfactory, they may return to the
open community. The point is that no placement is considered final, and that as circumstances change, the best
interests of the handicapped person may require a change in
the amount and type of supervision he receives. After some
years of steady employment and adjustment in marriage, it
seems reasonable to conclude that A is managing quite well
with the help of his wife, and needs to be seen only infre-
quently: supervision may be adequate for B while her parents
are alive, but on their death, she may need to be cared
for in an institution: C is very unstable in adolescence and
he and his parents need a lot of help, but as his situation
becomes more adjusted, so the frequency of the officer's
visits diminishes.

All of us have bad patches, but whereas most of us can be
left to get over them ourselves, or to find our own way to the
appropriate service (Home Help Office, Friendly Society, Sani-
tary Inspector, etc.), the handicapped person is likely to become bogged down by his difficulties or take an unacceptable
way out, such as theft or violence. It has been suggested that
many delinquent acts among subnormal young people could
be avoided with better use of the facilities available for
Community Care.

We may conclude that it is important that Medical Officers,

teachers in E.S.N. schools, and others whose opinions may carry weight when the decision to notify or not to notify is made, should be well-informed about the issues involved. If they all kept clearly before their minds that the provisions of the Mental Health Act are intended to ensure that help is always available to the handicapped person, and that it is a flexible help, they would be less likely to oppose notification on well-meaning but sentimental grounds, when it is in the interest of the child.

The practice of different Local Authorities varies greatly. In general, it is fair to say that the most progressive Authorities encourage the development of well-integrated voluntary schemes, but at the same time use their statutory powers when appropriate. It must be remembered that voluntary activities, however excellent, tend not to touch the most recalcitrant and these may be just the ones who can least safely be left to their own devices. With this proviso, that voluntary schemes cannot be expected to cover the problem alone, there is much to be said in favour of after-care of an informal kind, as when, for instance, E.S.N. schools keep in touch with their old pupils. Teachers who give up time in the evenings in this way are performing a valuable social service. At the same time, they should remember that what they are doing is of its nature limited, and should be ready to welcome, rather than greet with suspicion and distrust, the efforts of the social worker under the Mental Health Act. The end they both try to serve, the welfare of these handicapped young people, can best be served if they co-operate rather than by rivalry and competition and pretending that notification is unnecessary.

The teacher can reflect that, excellent as his efforts are, there are other people with other skills and other powers who can help the children in ways which are beyond his own competence; and that therefore it is folly to adopt an unduly proprietary attitude towards a child who was once in his care, but who by the mere fact of growing up has gone forward into a wider sphere. To go into the problems of adulthood with the mental equipment of a child—that is the hub of the difficulty; and the conscientious teacher can be only too thankful when he knows that there are sources of aid to which the handicapped young adult can turn.

In its Jubilee report, the Special Services After-Care Sub-Committee of the City of Birmingham gave an interesting account of the changes in policy in the treatment of the mentally handicapped over fifty years, and it concluded:

'It has enlarged and its nature has in some ways changed, but the main principles on which we base our work today are little altered—(1) to assist all employable persons to find suitable work; (2) to provide training centres where all unemployable persons can learn happily and develop to the full their limited capabilities; (3) to give help and advice where required; (4) to foster the right attitude towards mentally handicapped persons.'

This was written before the passage of the Mental Health Act, and it is still applicable, although some progress has been made in each respect. The number of sheltered workshops has increased, facilities for the rehabilitation and training of handicapped young adults have greatly improved, and generally, as was mentioned on p. 67, a much more optimistic view is taken of the potential employability of even some quite severely subnormal men and women. More is being done, both by the Ministry of Labour and by voluntary efforts locally (of which the best known are the successful experiments at Slough), to encourage integration within the community. The number of clubs and associations for the handicapped is increasing, and hobbies and leisure time interests are encouraged. Most important, the attitude of ordinary people towards the mentally handicapped is improving, though much still remains to be done to improve it further and remove lingering elements of the old attitude of 'shut them up—they're dangerous' and 'we don't want to know'. Parents' associations have played a great part in educating the public towards a more sympathetic attitude, and in reducing the burden of isolation, misplaced guilt and worry imposed on their members, but there is still no room for complacency, as they are the first to insist. The handicapped need tolerance and sympathy—they also need very practical help.

CHAPTER VII

The Setting and Scope of the Problem in Ordinary Schools

———

I T is much harder to discuss special educational treatment in ordinary schools than in special schools for many reasons. There is such a wide range of conditions, in size of classes, number on roll, equipment, and environment, that generalisations must constantly be qualified by reference to the conditions in which they apply. The organisation of ordinary schools is directed towards other purposes in addition to the furthering of special educational treatment: and whereas in a special E.S.N. school it can be taken for granted that its aim is single, backwardness is one only among the considerations that have to be taken into account in the ordinary school. Teachers in ordinary schools have other concerns and responsibilities, and many are not specially interested in slow children. In the ordinary school, backwardness is more protean and less clearly defined than it is in the E.S.N. school, so that our problem itself splits up into a number of sub-problems, ranging from a small minority whose difficulties are as great as those of children in E.S.N. schools, through a large minority whose difficulties are less acute though still serious enough, to a third group whose difficulties in learning are not so much inherent as acquired, and therefore in principle remediable. Above all, the numbers to be catered for are so much greater, that administrators can easily despair of making much impression—it is more rewarding to concentrate on piecemeal schemes for oppor-

tunity classes for a few children here and there, which are useful as far as they go but leave the main reservoir untouched.
Perhaps the problem of catering adequately for mentally handicapped children is soluble—I believe it is—but what about the
large army of the dull? Of course, it is no argument against
doing *something* that it doesn't cover *everything,* for a start in
one direction can afterwards be used and applied in others:
indeed it can be argued that that is what has happened in
England, and that the line of development in time is from a
limited provision for seriously handicapped children to the
much wider commitments for providing special educational
treatment that are now part of the duty of Local Education
Authorities. However that may be, the duty is there—and
also the difficulties and the opportunities that go with it.

Let us take some representative points of view concerning
backward children in ordinary schools in order to see what
assumptions are made and what issues are involved, as a preliminary to clearing the ground.

Administrator A. We are well ahead with our plans for
special educational treatment. We've already started two opportunity classes and six more are planned when we can get
the teachers. Then each area of the town will be covered. We'll
keep the numbers in the classes down to fifteen.

Administrator B. We tried special classes in ordinary
schools, but they weren't a success. If the children need it, our
policy now is to send them to the E.S.N. school, otherwise they
stay where they are. Numbers?—quite all right, the E.S.N.
school isn't overpressed and we can usually squeeze an urgent
case in without much delay.

Administrator C. We're ready to approve schemes from
Head Teachers for special classes. Mind you, they've not to be
just C streams.

Head Teacher D. Can't do much because the school is so

overcrowded with this influx into the district, and we are the only secondary modern school. We've got four streams and try to keep the D classes' numbers down and see they get good teachers, but that's all.

Head Teacher E. Of course this is only a small school. Next year I shall have five classes for the seven to eleven range, so I hope to start a special class for backward children then. No, I haven't decided yet who will be taking it.

Head Teacher F. There *are* no backward children in my school.

Head Teacher G. Well, we did have a special class three years ago with a teacher who particularly wanted to do it, and that worked quite well, but she left and we couldn't find anyone else to take it, so it had to be disbanded. The children? they were absorbed back in the other classes. No, we have no special educational treatment at present. We just have the ordinary four streams, five in the first year.

Any Teacher X. Backward class? Not likely!

It is worth while to disentangle the ideas that are taken for granted in these statements and in particular to discover what is meant by 'special class'.

1. A very common use of the phrase 'special class' is merely numerical. Many schools (e.g. junior, secondary modern) contain a four-year-age range, and multiples of four classes give a basic pattern of one-stream, two-stream and so on. But if the numbers on roll are such that five, nine or thirteen classes are required, the additional class is often called a special class. A better phrase would be the 'extra class', as it may very often be nothing more than that, and it tends to come into existence and to disappear as the numbers on roll fluctuate. This may seem a very trite statement, but the 'numerical' confusion occurs with surprising frequency in practice. It is a good example of the way in which words bedevil our thinking—'backward children

need *special* attention' and 'this is a *special* class' may very well be using the word 'special' in two quite distinct senses. An approximate translation of the first would be 'skilled' or 'unusually careful', but the second may mean anything. It could mean 'the class in which this skilled and unusually careful attention is given', and whatever it does in fact mean, it often carries with it a halo from this interpretation. The halo may not be deserved, but if one listens carefully to conversations of teachers and administrators the assumption can often be seen lurking that there is something meritorious in having a special class, which is lacking in a mere C stream class. So there may be: it all depends on how much there really is special about it (in the sense of 'skilled'). But it is fatally easy in using the same word to slide over from one sense to another without noticing.

Let us agree to avoid using the word 'special' in the merely numerical sense and call it an extra class. An extra class may: (*a*) be constituted for other reasons and contain backward children just incidentally, e.g. a bulge class, or one following a sudden influx into the district; (*b*) contain backward children only, and do nothing in particular about them; (*c*) contain backward children only, and make a genuine attempt to provide an education suited to their needs.

Recalling the remark of Head Teacher E, we may now translate his words as follows: 'Next year he will have an extra class, and it will be either Type (*b*) or Type (*c*)—we haven't enough information to tell us which. We hope it will be (*c*), but it all sounds rather haphazard, so we fear it may turn out to be (*b*).'

2. The next distinction is between arrangements for backward children which are haphazard, and those which are a genuine attempt at solution (*b* and *c* in the foregoing paragraph). Only in the latter sense can we talk of 'special educational treatment'. Remembering that we must not be misled by numerical considerations, we will be careful not to equate this distinction with one between special classes and C streams.

We can imagine a school where there happen to be four classes of backward children (and others where there happen to be three, two or one). Great care has been taken to work out suitable schemes for the classes, and the teachers try with some success to adopt differing approaches to fit the needs of individuals. In such cases, irrespective of the nomenclature of the classes or of their numbers in each school, we would say that special educational treatment was being given. Equally clearly, it is not special educational treatment when the C classes in a school merely do a watered down version of the A stream syllabus, or when an 'extra' class is working with no particular aim or purpose that distinguishes it from the rest of the school. In short, it is what goes on inside the room, and not the label on the door, that matters.

When Administrator C is speaking of the plans of his Authority, he means 'We want some really good teaching. We don't want anything rule of thumb.' Unfortunately, he words it in terms of special classes and C streams and this may be misleading, both to the Head Teachers in his district and to himself, if they and he are led to think that merit lies, of its nature, in an 'extra class' type of organisation for backward children. It seems that Head Teacher G thinks so, for he apparently assumes that now his 'extra' class has been disbanded the game is lost. The class may or may not have been a good one—quite probably it was, since the teacher's attitude was favourable—but the school is large and has need to make quite extensive arrangements for special educational treatment. It is doubtful whether the one class, even when it was operating, was sufficient. One hopes he is wrong when he said there is now no special educational treatment—as there must be at least four classes of backward children—but one fears he is right. He seems rather confused as to the size of his problem and also how to deal with it.

3. On the other hand, Head Teacher D does seem to be

doing what he can to help his backward children. He tries to keep the classes small, and to choose good teachers. He doesn't claim very much, but it may be quite sound as far as it goes. It is instructive to compare his conception of the size of the problem with that of some of the others. He takes for granted—rightly, in my opinion—that he has to make arrangements for quite a large minority of the children, say nearly one-quarter of the total roll. This very fact that the numbers are so large limits what facilities it is feasible to provide, so on a superficial view it is no wonder that his ideas seem somewhat pedestrian compared, for instance, with those of Administrator A. Administrator A's words may be interpreted in two ways. First, they may mean that (like Administrator C) he is anxious to have an altogether new attack on the question of providing special educational treatment, and to break away from the old routine lock-step. For this reason, he wants to experiment on a small scale, and find out what works in practice, and then extend it as required, modifying where necessary to meet the needs of large numbers. He does not think it wise to begin on a large scale, but proceeds cautiously from small beginnings. If this is what he means, well and good. But, secondly, he may mean that, having set up his eight classes, he is prepared to sit back content. In this case, 120 children out of a total school population of perhaps 20,000 are being catered for, and one wonders what happens to the remainder. It is noticeable, too, that he is claiming for his opportunity classes a more generous staffing standard than that of the special E.S.N. school in his area, and this is not easy to defend. On the former interpretation, he is far-sighted, but on the latter, it all sounds rather unrealistic.

The third distinction which is implicit in all this, is between quality and quantity. It stands to reason that it is easier to make a good standard of provision where numbers are limited: for instance, if a Head Teacher has one unusually good teacher who is anxious to work with backward children, the easy path for him would be to form one backward class only, leave the rest alone, and invite congratulations on the excellent stand-dard that has been attained. To persuade three other less gifted teachers to join in widens the scope, but it also dilutes the im-pressiveness of the performance. Yet in fact all large schools have enough backward children to fill more than one class. The difficulty is to find sufficient teachers to cover the need (remem-ber, for instance, the remark of teacher X). It is certainly no criticism of Adminstrator A that he is trying to improve the quality of provision, but only that he seems rather blind to the quantity required. If we constantly remind ourselves that in an average neighbourhood about one-sixth of all pupils are suffi-ciently dull to need a modified curriculum, and that about one-tenth come within the official definition of educationally sub-normal, we shall be nearer to the mark.

4. The fourth distinction that I should like to make is be-tween special educational provision and suitable educational provision. It is sometimes said that the ordinary fare provided in schools is not as suitable as it might be for the majority of children. An unduly bookish approach, particularly associated with the eleven plus examination, still prevails in many schools, especially in the formative years between seven and eleven. The range and number of topics covered and the manner of treatment is often determined by the claims of the examination rather than by the needs and interests of the children, yet only a minority is likely to proceed to selective secondary education. The majority adapt themselves as best they can, which in some cases means they do not adapt at all. In this I am not thinking only of very slow and dull children, who would require special arrangements whatever the circumstances, but of that large group of somewhat below average children who become bored and apathetic, one might almost say unnecessarily. In this sense it might be said that, were the ordinary education more *suitable*

for the great majority, there would be less need of special educational treatment, and particularly where remedial measures are concerned. There will, of course, always be need for special educational treatment for a minority of handicapped children, but it is as well to remind ourselves that more lasting good can be achieved for more children by improving the ordinary arrangements than by special measures which are of their nature limited. Smaller classes in the primary schools, to prevent avoidable backwardness, is one obvious reform, and is preferable from every point of view, to concentrating remedial measures on very retarded seniors. Since the well-known words in the Ministry's Report on the Primary School were written that 'the curriculum is to be thought of in terms of activity and experience rather than of knowledge to be acquired and facts to be stored'[1] the junior school curriculum is becoming less hidebound, but the process could with advantage be carried further. Again, and in some ways most important, is the question of teacher's attitudes (see, for example, the dictum of Head Teacher F). Where teachers are not willing to recognise and allow for individual differences in interest and aptitude, and where their goals are set too narrowly on one type of academic result, a large number of dullish children will be likely to flounder and become disheartened, and the number of those who require 'special' treatment will be correspondingly increased: on the other hand, teachers who are prepared to accept the children for what they are and to interest themselves in their general development and not only in their scholastic progress, can be said to be providing 'suitable' educational treatment.

It would be unfortunate if interest in special educational treatment led us to underestimate the great importance of the general suitability of the ordinary fare provided. The more flexible the approach of the ordinary classes (e.g. on return after absence), the less need there will be for special measures,

[1] Report of the Consultative Committee on the Primary School, para. 75.

apart from those necessitated by the inherent limitations of the children.

An example from another country may make the point at issue clearer. A city prides itself on its arrangements for mentally handicapped children, and indeed the percentage of such children attending special schools ($1 \cdot 8$) is high. It is true that this includes a number of children who would in England be considered ineducable, but even when these are subtracted the remainder ($1 \cdot 5$ per cent) is higher than most English authorities are able to secure. The difficulty is, that outside the special schools special treatment ceases altogether, and a child must conform to the ordinary regime (rather *more* academic than in most present day English schools, and without the streaming arrangements we are accustomed to in England which do at least lighten the burden on the non-academic child). It is either the special school or nothing, and one can imagine the plight of the dull under such conditions. A large, undifferentiated 'normal' group is set over against a small 'subnormal' minority: contrast this with the more fluid conception which the 1944 Act encourages in England, where degrees of subnormality are admitted and the special school shades over into the special class, and the special class into the various streams. Too much overlapping may be undesirable, but rigid demarcations can be more so. As I see it, the trend of development of special provision in England has been to start with the most gravely handicapped and gradually extend the scope— thus special schools came first, and then special classes. That is the stage we have reached at present, but it is interesting to speculate how much further the process of diversification can be carried within the ordinary schools, and at what point 'special' will cease to be special, and become 'suitable'. At any rate, although for convenience a distinction is made here between the two, it is not intended to imply that they are really in opposition—quite the reverse.

In the light of these comments, we may now turn to consider the statement of Administrator B. What he is saying in effect is, that having provided a special school, he has done all that is required. Here everything turns on the suitability of the ordinary schools. If every school is so well regulated that it can cater adequately for the varying abilities and aptitudes of all its pupils so that there is no need to provide special arrangements because 'specialness' has been swallowed up in 'suitability' as the greater includes the less, he is indeed to be congratulated. But is this ideal so easily attainable? A visit to some of these schools may lead one to doubt it. One has only to look very superficially to find many backward children who are not receiving much help, and who in some cases are very similar to the children in the E.S.N. school. Can it be that, on the contrary, the appearance of equilibrium is obtained only by imperfect ascertainment? (recall, for example, his statement that there is no pressure on the E.S.N. school and that numbers are adequate). It would appear likely that he is an example of the earlier stage of evolution we have discussed, where an undifferentiated normal group is contrasted with a small subnormal minority, and where it is either the special school or nothing.

5. Finally, the climate of opinion in the ordinary schools is of great importance in determining the extent and adequacy of the treatment provided there for backward pupils. Head Teachers who, like F, find it necessary to deny even the existence of the problem, and teachers who, like X, want to avoid teaching dull children, are all too common and in their presence it is unlikely that the educational treatment will be either suitable or special. Further witness to this point of the shortage of willing teachers can be gained from Administrator A and from Head Teacher G.

In the light of all the foregoing, it seems wise to consider the position of backward children who are not receiving special educational treatment, as well as those who are. I propose, therefore, next to consider what one may call the 'ordinary' set-up in schools of various sizes where backward children may be found. In some of these, the very small ones, the conditions are such as to preclude the possibility of their ever making special provision for one or two backward children. Where this is so, the fact must be respected, but even so it is worth while thinking of ways in which the best use can be made of the assets, while minimising the disadvantages, of the very small school. In other schools or groups of schools, there is no reason in principle why special educational treatment could not be provided, so that after discussing the probable extent of the need for provision in medium and large schools, we turn to the main task of considering the various ways in which such special educational treatment may be organised, with the advantages and disadvantages of each.

CHAPTER VIII

'Ordinary' Educational Treatment

A. *Very Small Schools*

I N one sense it seems almost a contradiction in terms to discuss very small schools in a book which is avowedly concerned with the organisation of special educational treatment. A case can be made for arguing that none of the children can possibly receive special treatment, if by that is meant elaborate arrangements, or alternatively that all the children do, since their work is bound to be individualised. Certainly no highly organised measures are possible, but since there are children who are backward in schools of all sizes, and teachers who have to help the children whatever the conditions, the very small schools cannot be omitted from consideration. They have their own particular difficulties but they also have their own particular opportunities. These will be summarised in turn.

The teacher-in-charge, who may or may not have an assistant, has between fifteen and thirty-five children on the roll. Some of the very small schools have been closed altogether and others have been decapitated so that they now take children up to eleven, but even so the age range in the class is considerable, though the numbers in the class are small by town standards. Let us take as example a class of fifteen children aged five to eleven with one teacher working single-handed. Her main preoccupations include Bill and Bobby, aged five and six, who are always fighting, May and Victor who will be leaving in July and are due to take the General Examination next month, Myrtle who is eight and brighter than any of the others, Betty who is nine and in a town would certainly be in an E.S.N. school, and Vera aged ten who is having a bad patch of bossiness: the remainder are her minor preoccupations and at any moment can become major. Myrtle and possibly Victor are above average: eight are more or less of average ability, but they are of all ages and include the troublesome Vera and Bill: four are definitely slow, but three of these are stolid; Bobby is both dull and naughty and finally there is Betty. At least the teacher can reflect that the mongol from the Crossways is still only four! she is not looking forward to next year when he will join Bill and Bobby. In this setting, Betty presents a problem, certainly, but in another way so does Myrtle, so do Bobby, Bill and Vera. The teacher's task is not only to cater suitably for Betty and the other slow children, but to do it in a context where the needs of the others also have to be considered, and where mental handicap is one only among a wide range of problems. All the children have some claim on her attention, and several have a particular claim for a variety of reasons: it is evident that Betty cannot receive more than a share of the attention, for her claim, though it is 'particular', is not more so than several of the others. The teacher wrote to the County Offices about Betty some time ago, but no action has been taken yet. The present situation is that Betty can print her name and recognise it, but can recognise no other words with certainty. She is still using apparatus with her Introductory Book: she can count up to ten and do additions using concrete material. There is no question of her working with Myrtle who is nearest to her in age: occasionally Myrtle will join with Vera and May, but the grouping is very fluid and in general all have their own work to do and get on with it at their own rate. In this way, although Betty is working individually, so are the others, and if her pace is slow, at least it is her own pace and she is not being dragged forward as she might be in a large unit. She is not receiving special educational treatment, but she is fitting in, in a fashion, and learning a little, and it is difficult to see what more can be done until she goes, if ever she does go, to the residential E.S.N. school.

The drawbacks of the situation are obvious, but there can be some advantages over a corresponding situation in a town school.

1. She is working at her own pace and not at one dictated by the need to fit in with a group standard.

2. She has the advantage of an easily comprehensible environment, both in school and out. The pace and complexity of life in a large city can be utterly beyond the understanding of a subnormal child who feels himself whirled along on an impersonal organisation—where father goes, what he does for a living, the very name of his job may be unknown; whereas in the country the routines are related to needs and tasks which can be understood by a child.[1]

3. The school is smaller and more of a family affair, and not a large organised machine which swallows children at nine and disgorges them at four. Whether the 'family' school is a happy one or not is a very pertinent question (and depends largely on the teacher), but at its best it can provide a natural atmosphere that is not unduly threatening to a handicapped child, as even a well-run large community may be.

4. Whether a handicapped child fits in or is singled out seems to depend on a number of factors including his temperament, the tone of the group and the extent of his handicap. Even a severely handicapped child is sometimes well accepted by his fellows and treated with tolerance, while another is a butt. Betty, it so happens, is accepted in spite of her handicap. When this happens, the fact that she is working alongside the others, in the same room with no singling out, can be helpful in developing confidence. On the other hand, one who is rejected can be harmed by similar proximity, if it merely means

[1] This is well brought out by 'Miss Read' in *Village School*.

that the others rub in his limitations. Here again the attitude of the teacher is important in setting the tone.

5. The mixture of age groups can be utilised to advantage. This has been pointed out in connection with E.S.N. schools and will not be dealt with further here.

6. The teacher really knows the children and their families, and the importance of this knowledge cannot be overestimated. It has been said that easier transport makes it increasingly possible for teachers to live elsewhere, and the moving away of teachers (especially the men, as the schools are decapitated) raises social issues which are too wide for the present discussion,[1] but it is still fair to say that the country teacher usually has a more genuine knowledge of the children and their homes than her town counterpart. This knowledge is useful at all levels, but it is particularly important where backward children are concerned.

It is fair to conclude that there may be advantages for the social development of backward children in a village school compared with a town one, at least in their early years. From an educational point of view, practices which are less efficient in drilling average and bright children to a degree of proficiency may be no drawback to a backward child, and be outweighed by the advantage to him of being able to follow his own pace more than would be possible in a more highly organised environment.

All this is simply to say that a good small school may be a not unsuitable place for educationally subnormal children; but village schools are rather like the girl with the curl 'when they're good, they're very, very good, but when they're bad, they're horrid'.

B. *Larger Village Schools*, with 90 to 120 children on roll, and three or four classes to cater for a six-year age range (re-organ-

---

[1] See, for example, Orwin, *Country Planning*; Parkyn, *The Consolidation of Rural Schools*.

ised) or a ten-year range (un-reorganised). Here again much that was said earlier applies regarding the relative difficulties and opportunities. It is obvious that in a class with a two- or three-age range the teacher will have her hands full to organise the work of the different groups, and will be unable to make thorough-going special arrangements for individuals. In such a situation, the dull children will be among the oldest in the class, but they will be doing the work of the youngest group present. This may work up to a point with some of the less seriously backward children, but a really mentally handicapped child is likely to find that the pace even of the youngest group is faster than his; if, for example, Frank is ten years old with a mental age of six-and-a-half, and the class contains children of chronological ages eight, nine, and ten. To put him into a lower class would raise additional difficulties unless he is extremely puny and babyish for his age, and so it may become a choice of evils. Much depends on his own temperament and on the readiness of the other children nearest to him in age to accept him, and this comes back again to the climate within the class and the example of acceptance set by the teacher. Again, the fact that he is working in the same room, though not in the same group, as children of similar age may be helpful or may be the reverse, according to circumstances. 'A child cannot be more cruelly segregated than to be placed in a room where his failures separate him from other children who are experiencing success.'[1] A teacher who is critical of his poor attempts can underline his segregation, while another who is ready to praise him for effort and to find tasks for him that are within his competence so that he can feel an integral part of the class, minimises the consciousness of difference that lies at the root of segregation. Paradoxically, the larger numbers compared with the tiny school of the foregoing section, as they

[1] *National Society for the Study of Education*, 49th Year Book, Part II, p. 24.

make group teaching in the three R's possible (each section of the class may contain up to ten or twelve children) may be a disadvantage to Frank in so far as they cause the teacher to rely overmuch on group instruction. Individual work, which was a commonplace for all in the tiny school, may be something out of the ordinary here, and so emphasise his disability. This is a risk that may have to be taken, for to fail at the eight-year-old work would be worse still, and it can be minimised if the teacher is tactful regarding any separate work which she manages, in spite of the other claims on her attention, to devise for Frank. At least it can be said that it is easier for her to borrow and adapt suitable materials from the teacher of younger children next door than for a teacher similarly placed with an educationally subnormal ten-year-old in a large town junior school, where the infant department is entirely separate and the co-operation between the two departments is none too good! Here again there is need for tact in borrowing or devising materials which, though suitable in level of difficulty, are not so patently babyish as to be a source of amusement to the other children and of shame to Frank.

As Frank gets older, he is more likely to come within the purview of special arrangements, either by transfer with all the other children at eleven plus to a modern school in a neighbouring town or central village, or possibly to a residential E.S.N. school. The retention of children beyond the age of eleven in village schools is nowadays much questioned: an excellent discussion of the issues raised is to be found in G. W. Parkyn's report for the New Zealand Council for Educational Research, *The Consolidation of Rural Schools.* Although he writes of New Zealand much of what he says is applicable to other countries, and the simple device by which he tests the width of social contact of the children is particularly interesting. He concludes that for young children a good small school has much to commend it, but that even the best small school is too restricted in its possibilities, not only of scholastic progress, but also of the development of social interests, to meet the diverse needs of older children. How much of this is applicable when we turn from the normal to the subnormal adolescent is debatable. Certainly the provision of suitable separate work for Frank and his like, which is difficult enough when he is young, becomes much more so when he is older, if he remains in an unreorganised school. On the other hand, the argument in favour of transfer to a centrally placed larger school, that it allows of wider social contacts, is of less importance for a subnormal child, and indeed it may be said that the simpler local contacts are more easily comprehended by him than a wider circle which, though beneficial to average children, may be confusing to him. Of course, it is impossible to generalise, as much depends on the temperament and sociability of each child, and also on the adequacy of his adjustment to his original village school. Where an evidently subnormal child remains in an unreorganised school after the age of eleven, it is certainly desirable that the County Authority be warned of his presence, so that even if he cannot be sent to a residential E.S.N. school, there is a possibility of enlisting specialist help and advice (e.g. from the Authority's psychologists or from the peripatetic advisers or teachers that some Authorities are appointing) and so that, on leaving school, he can be reported if necessary to the Mental Health Authority as needing care and supervision.

C. *One Stream Schools* in large villages, small and big towns, and cities. This often (by no means always) turns out to be the most unfavourable situation of all from our standpoint of the adequacy of the help that can be given to backward children within the ordinary framework of the school. This may seem odd, as the difficulties of organisation are apparently less than those in smaller schools, yet in practice such a school often has its own great difficulties. To begin with, the classes are larger than those in many village schools, where in fixing the staffing ratio allowance is made for the greater age range within a class. The range of ability in a single class may be very wide and even though the children are all ten by the calendar, their mental ages may easily vary from less than seven to thirteen or more. In such a situation group work in the basic subjects is essential, but not always carried out. A not very good teacher who, if she had a class of mixed ages, would realise that she should deal with the sevens and eights separately, is often liable to overlook a *mental* age range which is far greater, and attempts to teach the class as a homogeneous unit. In such a situation, she may aim for the average and then the extremes are neglected; or, remembering the claims of the eleven plus examination, she pitches her requirements rather high for the majority and the slower children are more than ever left behind. Of course, there are many exceptions to this, and teachers who manage to diversify their approach even under the unfavourable conditions of a large class with a maximum mental age range, but my point is just that the conditions *are* particularly unfavourable. Again, these schools which are small by urban standards, are often old and badly housed and equipped. If a building is unattractive and dingy and on the verge of the black list those responsible are often unwilling to spend money on it, arguing that it will sooner or later be closed. It may be a church school and suffer from shortage of funds, or it may be the Local Authority's Cinderella. Enterprising teachers not unnaturally find newer and brighter schools more attractive and a vicious circle then forms which it is hard to break.

At the same time, it is worth remembering that a *good* voluntary school may be a very happy place, even if the building is deplorable. Such a school is often more successful in gaining the interest and loyalty of the parents (they may themselves have attended it) than the brand new crystal palace down the road, and when the church and the teachers work together harmoniously for the welfare of the children (they do not always do so), an excellent 'family' atmosphere is sometimes achieved.[1] In this way, the smallness of the school, by town standards, may itself become an asset. It is probable that there will not be separate infant and junior departments, and the children continue in the same environment from five to eleven. If the environment is an unhappy one, this is a pity, but if it is reasonably happy, it means that the children can be well known to their teachers, and while this is important for all children, it is particularly important for those who are backward or subnormal. It is wise, then, not to overstate the harmful effect of poor material conditions, though equally they should not be ignored, nor should it be assumed too readily that the happy atmosphere of which we have spoken does in fact exist! Leaving all these on one side, we are left with the inescapable facts that each class does contain a very wide ability range and that the classes are large: and taken together these are a serious drawback. There is a very good case for Authorities to be ready to increase the staffing ratio in such schools: they should not be treated on a par with the average large town or city school. As things are, there is some suggestion that they contribute more than their fair share to the *avoidable* cases of backwardness that afterwards come needing remedial work to the secondary modern schools. On this point, it is impossible to generalise as the schools differ so among themselves and also we must bear in mind the varying quality of their material; there are some which attain a remarkably even level of performance allowing for the calibre of the children: others which drill their brighter children while the slower ones stagnate and leave more backward than they need have been; and others

[1] Statistical confirmation of this is given in the article by Kemp 'Environmental and other characteristics determining Attitudes in Primary Schools', in the *British Journal of Educational Psychology*, June 1955. He found that children's interest in their school was greater in small, old, voluntary schools than in new good buildings.

which are rather poor all round—it would be rather surprising if there were not, when we remember the unfavourable conditions. At any rate, it is fair to say that special educational treatment is not possible in such circumstances, and that when the 'ordinary' conditions become too unsuitable, further backwardness may result, beyond that which is due to the inherent limitations of the children. If it can keep this additional backwardness down to a minimum, then the one-stream school has done all that can reasonably be expected.

For the teacher who has to work with such a class, it may be helpful to indicate in a general way the extent and range of mental variation which is likely to be encountered, using the principle of the normal curve of distribution. I have frequently found that to discuss variability in terms of Mental Ages provides a good rough guide on which to work. Many teachers find I.Q.'s rather too abstract a conception to be helpful in practice, whereas to speak of Mental Ages has the advantage that it provides a rough general indication as to the level of development that can be expected of the children. 'Treat as Mental Age' is a useful first approximation that is simple and readily understood—as long as it is remembered that it is an approximation only, and that a child should not be expected to conform in every respect—educational, social and emotional —to its theoretical standard. Nevertheless, such as it is, it is an improvement on the naïve view of children which takes into account only the date of their birth, and provided its limitations are remembered it can be quite useful.

Two versions are appended: one for ten-year-old children in a primary school, and one for twelve-year-olds after selection has taken place. Although most schools for senior children are larger than one-stream, there are some where for special reasons (e.g. denominational) the size is limited to a one-form entry, and so for the sake of completeness it will be given as well.

Ten-year-old class: Number in class—40

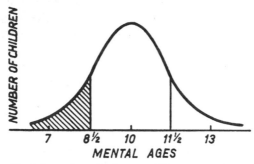

Fig. 1. Shaded portion = backward children = one-sixth of class.

TABLE I

Mental Ages	Below 7	7-8½	8½-10	10-11½	11½-13	13+
	M.H.	Dull	Average		Bright	V. bright
No. of Children	(1)	6	13	13	6	1

Notes

1. These figures are *approximate only* and may not represent the position in a given class. It must be realised that the properties of the normal curve of distribution, from which the expected proportions at different levels of Mental Age have been worked out, hold with accuracy only for large numbers. Of 1,000 children aged ten it is highly probable that two-thirds will have Mental Ages between eight and a half and eleven and a half, but when the numbers are small, selective factors exert a disproportionate effect. A single school, for instance, may be situated in an unusually prosperous or an unusually poor area and the distribution of Mental Ages will be skewed accordingly. Teachers should bear this in mind before trying to apply the proportions given to their own class, and should consider what relation their school bears to the other schools of the district, e.g. is it considered to be a school attended by many bright

children? In the light of this and similar considerations, the proportions given may need considerable correction, and it is wise always to think of them as suggestive only—suggestive of the amount and range of educational variability after which a programme for catering for these variations can be worked out in terms of the actual children in the class.

2. The previous remarks apply particularly to the numbers at the extremes of the range. One year there may be two or even three very bright children, and another year perhaps none at all. Every teacher can think of fluctuations such as this from year to year within his experience. In general, in an 'average' school in an average district, and taking one year with another, he may expect to find about one-sixth of his total group to be slow and dull—in a class of forty, that is, about seven—and of these, an occasional child may be found to be mentally handicapped.

3. Brackets have been placed round the entry '1' in the mentally handicapped column, as the child or children concerned may or may not have been discovered and transferred to the E.S.N. school. It is highly desirable that Authorities should make a special attempt to discover and transfer those of mentally handicapped level who are attending schools in which there is but one class for each age group, as there is no likelihood of their receiving special educational treatment while they remain there (as might be possible in a larger school) and their presence is an additional strain on a teacher who is already overburdened if he is attempting conscientiously to differentiate his approach to meet the needs of his widely varying pupils.

4. The proportions may be helpful to the teacher in deciding the size of the groups into which he splits his class for work, e.g. in number. The middle group of average children is likely to be the largest: the very brightest and the very slowest may require individual work, and so on. Obviously for project work

groups of more equal size and containing children with a varied range of talents would be needed.

5. It is hardly necessary to add that this approach sounds unduly rigid and stereotyped. A good teacher thinks not in terms of categories but of living children—Doreen and Elizabeth and William. Nevertheless, it can help him to reflect on the probable level of Doreen's capacity as compared with that of the others, if he knows the amount of variation to expect and allow for, and this is all that is being suggested here. I am thinking here not so much of the experienced teacher who instinctively alters his approach to fit the needs of individuals, but of the beginner who needs to have a rough guide or crutch to help him.

Twelve-year-old class: Number in class—32

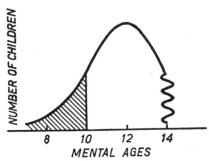

Fig. 2. Shaded portion = backward children = nearly one quarter of class.

TABLE 2

Mental Ages	below 8	8-10	10-12	12-14	14+
	M.H.	dull	average		bright
No. of children	(1)	6	12	12	1

Notes

1. Previous notes apply.

2. The class of thirty-two represents a truncated portion of an original distribution of forty, from which the top 20 per cent

have been removed by the selection examination at eleven. The truncation is represented by a wavy line rather than a clean break to show that there may be some overlapping in ability between the weakest who have gone to the grammar school and the brightest of those who remain.

3. The proportion of backward children is greater than in a corresponding class of juniors.

D. *Larger Schools*. Once the number of children in an age group is more than can be contained in a single class, it is common in England to make some sort of differentiation on an ability, or at least an attainment basis. In this way it is hoped to render the task of teaching large numbers easier since the spread in any one class is reduced. Many teachers think of the resulting classes as being homogeneous enough to teach as a unit, but this is far from being the case, even in quite large schools of three or more streams, particularly where the extremes are concerned. It is instructive to see the surprising differences that do in fact remain, and need to be taken into account in the teacher's planning.

Two-stream schools: Ten-year-old classes: Number in each class—40

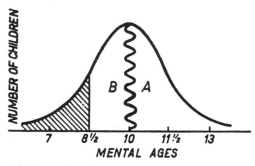

Fig. 3. Shaded portion = backward children = one-third of B class.

TABLE 3

		below 7	7-8½	8½-say 11
B Class	Mental Age	below 7	7-8½	8½-say 11
	No. of children.	(1 or 2)	12	26
A Class	Mental Age	say 9-11½	11½-13	13+
	No. of children.	26	12	2

Notes

1. See previous notes.

2. For the sake of simplicity, round figures have been taken. It has been assumed that there are exactly eighty children for the two classes, and that they have been split equally. In practice such convenient age groupings are not always found! and also many Head Teachers try to keep their A classes larger than the B classes. But even if the numbers were say forty-three and thirty-seven, it would not affect the general picture much, so it seemed wisest for clarity to show a symmetrical distribution. The easiest way for a teacher to make a correction for his own class of thirty-seven, is to assume that he still has all the very slow children and simply subtract the number required from the top group (in this case he would take away three from twenty-six).

3. Some overlapping in the middle between the classes is always found in practice, and is probably inevitable. There is not a perfect correlation between children's ability and their attainments, while absence, home background, industry, coaching, etc., all effect an influence, and schools are not always able to avoid erroneous placements based on mistaken judgments of children's capacity. So it is likely that the B class will contain some children who are actually a bit above average, and abler than the weakest of the A's. It is certainly wrong to consider, as some teachers still do, the B class as containing nothing but backward children.

4. The proportion of backward children in the B class has gone up to one-third, i.e. a sizeable fraction of the total.

5. Although the spread of ability in each class has been reduced somewhat as compared with a one-stream class, it is still large. Note in particular that it has *not* been halved, as one might at first suppose, on account of the overlapping. The range is similar in each class, unless the very handicapped children at the bottom end have been transferred to an E.S.N. school. *Twelve-year-old classes*: Number in each class—32

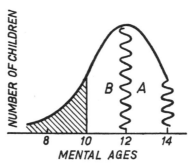

Fig. 4. Shaded portion = backward children = nearly half of B class.

TABLE 4

B. Class	Mental Age	below 8	8-10	10-say 12+
	No. of children	(2)	12	18
A Class	Mental Age	say 10½-12	12 - 14	14+
	No. of children	6	24	2

Notes

1. See previous notes.

2. As the distribution is asymmetrical, the spread of ability is greater in the B class. (This is an additional reason to justify the practice of Head Teachers in keeping the B class smaller.)

3. Nearly half the B class are likely to be dull, and some of them may be very dull indeed.

Three-stream schools: Ten-year-old classes: Number in each class—40

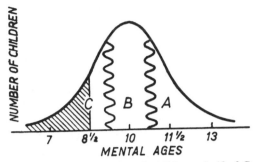

Fig. 5. Shaded portion = backward children = half of C class.

TABLE 5

C Class	Mental Age	below 7	7-8½	8½-say 10	
	No. of children	(3)	18	19	
B Class	Mental age			say 9-11	
	No. of children			40	
A Class	Mental age		say 10-11½	11½-13	13+
	No. of children		19	18	3

Notes

1. See previous notes.

2. The B class is relatively homogeneous, but both the A and the C classes still contain a fair spread of ability. The easiest class for a beginner to cater for is therefore the B class, and this fact can with advantage be considered by Head Teachers when deciding where to place a new teacher straight from college. There is little danger that he will want to place him with an A class, but in the past it has been a frequent practice to put beginners with the C classes, and this is difficult to defend. Leaving out of account the particular difficulties that such a teacher might encounter, the spread of ability alone is such as to make such a placement less suitable than that with a B class.

3. The proportion of dull pupils in the C class has now risen to half (and will be more than half if the Head Teacher tries as he probably does, to keep the numbers down). As it stands, this may not sound surprising, and perhaps it is best expressed the other way round, that even in a three-stream school a fair number of the children in the C classes are *not* dull. This may serve as a timely reminder to those who are wont to dismiss the C classes *in toto* with a shrug; but it also increases the teacher's responsibility since he has to do justice not only to his backward group (which contains by now a pretty heavy tail) but also to a sizeable group of low average children. In such circumstances, it is easy for the latter to become backward by default, if he sets his expectations too low for them. It cannot too often be repeated that, even in quite large schools, it is wrong to conceive of the classes at the extremes of the distribution as a homogeneous unit.

Twelve-year-old classes: Number in each class—32

TABLE 6

		below 8	8-10	10-say 11	
C class	Mental Age	below 8	8-10	10-say 11	
	No. of children	(3)	18	11	
B class	Mental Age			say 10½-12	12-say 13
	No. of children			25	7
A class	Mental Age			12-14	14+
	No. of children			29	3

Notes

1. See previous notes.

2. The majority of the C class are now backward and account for approximately two-thirds of the total.

3. The A and B classes are now relatively homogeneous, but the C class has a wider spread of ability than either. It still contains a few children who are not technically dull, but there is a long heavy tail.

Schools of four or more streams. It is not intended to continue to work out in detail the numbers of children of each mental age level that one might expect to find in each streamed class: those who need the information may work it out for themselves using the same general method and remembering, of course, that their results will be approximate only. The principles are that about one-sixth of an unselected group of child-

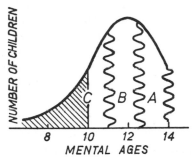

Fig. 6. Shaded portion = backward children = nearly two-thirds of C class.

ren are likely to be dull, and that as the number of streams increases, so does the weighting of the bottom stream with dull and handicapped children. Even without any official selection, each D or E stream class in a large school is likely to be to all intents and purposes a 'special' class, meaning by that that it is a class containing children whose need for special educational treatment is unquestionable. Whether or not they are getting it is, of course, another matter, but it is desirable to nail once and for all the notion that special educational treatment can be confined to a handful of children.

It will be realised that the account given here of the situation of backward children in schools of different sizes contains a number of omissions. The picture has been deliberately simplified, and no account has been taken of the not uncommon situation where there are half classes per age group, i.e.

six or ten classes in all, or where there are extra classes. Those who are particularly concerned with such a situation can make their own analysis of the extent of the problem in the various eventualities: in general, it is fair to say that any school of one-and-a-half streams or more is likely to have sufficient backward children to fill one class, though whether in a given case such children could or should all be gathered together from their various classes is another matter. I am not concerned to advocate this (the merits and demerits of such special classes will be considered later), but only to point out the size of the problem. Furthermore, no attempt has been made to consider other aspects of the handling of slow and dull children, beyond their class placement. This may give an unduly rigid impression, as if nothing matters beyond the basic subjects, performance in which usually determines a child's class placement: nothing has been said of the practical and aesthetic subjects of the curriculum, and not much of emotional development. It is by no means intended to imply that these can be safely ignored, but the scope has been deliberately limited in order to focus attention on the main point at issue—the numbers of children who are likely to need particular help, as and when it can be procured. Finally, it must be remembered that no account has here been taken of those children who become backward for causes other than limited ability. To avoid making the tables unduly complicated, it has been assumed that children of average ability or more just do not get into the C streams, yet this does in fact happen. To the problem of the slow and the dull, who will always need special help, is added a varying quantum of other children who require remedial help perhaps only for a time.

Here then, are the children. Whether they attend a small school or a large one, whether they are being catered for adequately or inadequately—in either case they remain, and their needs are the ultimate fact to be reckoned with.

CHAPTER IX

Methods of Providing Special Educational Treatment in Ordinary Schools

I T will be assumed in this chapter that, where practicable, special E.S.N. schools cater for the most gravely handicapped, and that special educational treatment in the ordinary schools is not thought of as a substitute for the special schools, but has as its main task the provision of suitable education for a relatively large number of dull children with whom academic methods must always fail. In some areas, where there are no day E.S.N. schools, some mentally handicapped children will perforce remain in the ordinary schools, but in general the functions of special classes and special schools should be thought of as complementary and not as inter-changeable. Our task now is to discuss the various ways in which special educational treatment may be organised, with the advantages and disadvantages of each.

I. THE SINGLE CLASS

This is the most familiar way of organising special education treatment, and is to be found at all levels of effectiveness. Obviously, there is no point in discussing here those that are a mere travesty, and so in what follows it will be assumed that the teacher is capable, kindly, and interested in his task, and that the children's co-operation has been gained.

Because this is a special class, and known as such, the teacher is in many respects much freer than his colleagues. He does not interlock with anybody, and so he does not have to worry about completing a prescribed part of the four-year school syllabus, before handing over his children to the next teacher. He is allowed greater latitude in ignoring bells than the majority of his colleagues, though he is expected to maintain a reasonable balance between different types of activity, but when and how he does this is his own concern. He is thus able to organise his work flexibly, taking full advantage of sudden accessions of interest on the part of his pupils when they occur. The fact that his children stay with him for two or three or sometimes four years means that he can get to know them really well; thus he can both fit in his teaching to their individual interests and requirements, and also pay a wider regard than the average teacher is able to do to their general social and emotional development. He can afford to bide his time, and wait patiently over a long period of apparent lack of progress, until confidence has been gained, and the timid child is ready to go forward. If he teaches in a secondary modern school, he may see the rest of the school caught up in an elaborate jigsaw of specialisation, from which he and his class are mercifully exempt, and because he keeps his children (with a few obvious specialist exceptions) all day and every day, he is able to exercise a guiding influence over all their class work and to see that it is properly integrated, not merely in a paper scheme, but in the minds of the children, so that they see what they are doing as a planned whole. From the children's point of view, it makes all the difference in the world that they are with a teacher who is prepared to accept them, as not all teachers do, and that by remaining with him they can increase their feeling of security.

The single class has, however, its drawbacks. An illuminating episode once occurred at a meeting of teachers. The teacher of the 'extra' class in a five class junior school (who was in fact genuinely trying to provide 'special' educational treatment) mentioned that she found it difficult to answer her pupils when they asked why they did not have so-and-so 'like the others'. Another teacher pounced on this, saying 'How is it that they *know* they're different?' She was completely confused, could not reply, and he scored an easy victory. But, of course, though few of us were quick enough to see it at the time, his point was purely a debating one: whatever she said or did the children could hardly fail to realise that they were different. If you belong to a class in which there is no promotion, so that you stay there for four years, in a school setting in which most other children move up into a different class each year, it stands to reason that whatever the teacher's efforts, the children must know they do not conform to the ordinary pattern. This leads to the question of stigma, on which it is very easy to talk pious nonsense. Many of the things that are sometimes said about labelling children can apply with equal effect not only to a special class, but also to C streams, coaching groups, E.S.N. schools, clinic visits, remedial teaching—in short to any and every attempt to provide special help for children who need it. Furthermore, if in fact the children *are* different, it does not help matters to try to shut our eyes to this and refuse to recognise it. The important thing is whether they are better or worse as a result of the special help, and if they are better to continue it as long as it is required irrespective of any bogey about 'stigma'. If this is the *only* way in which help can be given, the criticism is pointless; but it becomes relevant if there are alternative means of providing help which are not open to the same objections. In the case at issue here, to remain four years in the one class is not a drawback in a small village school, where everybody does it; but it can be a big drawback to social acceptance in a town school, where the usual promotion pattern is quite otherwise. Similar remarks apply to the question of mixed age groups—many people hold that to try to teach seven-year-olds and eleven-year-olds in the same class is undesirable. This is not to say that a skilful teacher may not make good use of social interplay among the children, using the older ones to help the younger, as in a family; but at least the objection needs consideration. If the only alternative to the seven to eleven class is to do nothing at all, and the children need special educational treatment, then obviously the objection cannot be sustained and the need must take precedence, but it is desirable to pause and consider the consequences and the alternatives before setting up *a priori* the single class as the *ideal* form of provision.

Leaving aside the question of stigma and the feeling of difference as being debatable, the four-year class nevertheless has to face considerable difficulties of organisation. The children are all at different stages, not only in their class work but in their physical and social development: this applies particularly to a single class in a secondary modern school. We can assume that marked difficulties such as bullying do not occur if the class is a good one, but nevertheless minor misfits between the needs of younger and older children are likely. The absence of promotion may lead to a feeling of stagnation and discouragement, both for teacher and pupils. It is necessary for the school to have a clear policy with regard to the class, whether it is intended as a permanent home for innately dull children, or whether it is conceived as having primarily a remedial function. Both functions are legitimate, but they cannot easily be carried out in the same class—yet in practice this frequently does happen. It is understandable that if Roger is admitted to school at the age of nine, having moved from hospital to convalescent home and back again for four years, the obvious placement for him is the special class, for however bright he is he has no school attainments, but the difficulty is that the other children may be of very different calibre. But the biggest drawback to the single class is that it fails to cover the extent of the need, unless the school is a small one. Take, for instance, the not uncommon situation where a single class exists in a school with 500 children on roll. However excellent it is, it is simply inadequate. What is really happening is that, out of the 130-odd children in each year group, special attention is being given to perhaps six or seven. In such a situation only the most markedly aberrant children are being helped—but there are likely to be at least eight or ten others whose difficulties are only slightly less. It is what happens to them in the C stream that is the crucial test. If the example of the freer syllabus of the special class infects the C streams and gradually influences them, well and good. But paradoxically what often seems to happen is that the more the special class is thought of as 'special', the more the other classes tend to think of themselves as 'ordinary'. Those in authority often act as if they thought that once there is a special class, that finishes the matter and there is no need to make any other adjustments in the general requirements of the school syllabus, and the attitude towards the C stream hardens. The distinction becomes one between the abnormal few and the normal majority: of providing something very *special* for a handful and perhaps becoming less *suitable* for the lower streams. The point is not an easy one to make, since it can easily be twisted into the absurdity of objecting to something that is good because there is not more of it. Agreed that it is no criticism of a good class that it cannot be made available to all, but the point at issue is the impact of the special class on the rest of the school. Is it, so to speak, the spearhead of a new onset on the problem? or is it just one pretty purple patch sewn on to the outside of a vastly different educational fabric? The hardest test of a special class is not to be found in its influence on its own children, but in its influence on the other teachers and on the general philosophy and outlook of the school. One sometimes hears stories of A class boys who visit the special class, admire its gadgets, and end by asking 'Can I come in this class?'—which doesn't say much for the work of the school. The reform of the A classes is (fortunately) not to be discussed here, but in all seriousness one suggests there is something wrong if there is wide disparity between the aims and achievements of the C classes and the special class. My point is only that the more a special class is set apart from the rest of the school, and is given, for instance, much smaller numbers and better equipment than the ordinary C classes, the less is it likely to act as a model. Do we *want* it to act as a model? is the crucial question to ask. If we think of special educational treatment in the ordinary school as being extra special, something that is needed by only a minority of markedly aberrant children, then there is no reason why it should spread. But on a wider view that the children who remain in the ordinary school are not usually markedly aberrant—otherwise they would be in the special school—special educational treatment is much more likely to be a matter of width, so to speak, rather than depth. In the terms of our example, not only the six or seven children in each age group who are in the special class receiving intensive help, but the eight or ten others at the bottom of each C class should come within our terms of reference. It is desirable that the special class should have good working conditions and adequate facilities, but if these mark it off too sharply from the rest of the school, the final effect may not be what the Authority fondly imagines it to be. The obvious retort of the not-very-good C class teacher is 'It's all very well for him to do that, with his small class, but I have forty in here. Anyway his children need special help, and mine don't'. Far from acting as a model, the effect in this case has been to underline differences and make them into a barrier, and to increase complacency ('mine don't need anything different').

I would hazard a guess that the popularity of the single class expedient stems, not so much from a careful thinking-through of the merits of this type of organisation, but from the unpopularity of the task of teaching backward children among many teachers. It is easier to find one teacher who will undertake the task than to find two or more, and so it is natural for the Head Teacher to think he can best solve his pressing problems if he forms but one class and fills it with those children from whatever age group whose presence in the other classes causes most clamour. The distinction here is between solving pressing problems and providing adequately for the needs of the children—including those dull quiet ones about whom there is no clamour.

I have given reasons for suggesting that the single class, by itself, is not really a solution, and that it raises its own difficulties of organisation to have a four-year age range in one class, when the general pattern of the school is quite different.

A preferable expedient is to have two special classes, each catering for two age groups only. The isolation of the class and its teacher is decreased: heterogeneity is reduced: the feeling of progress is restored by promotion: use can be made of differing approaches by the complementary gifts and tastes of the two teachers (providing, of course, their general framework is common): and twice as many children can be given the benefit. The special educational treatment provided will be less intensive cultivation, something set apart, but it will be more extensive.

The difficulty arises when two suitable teachers cannot be found, or when only one extra class can be formed with the numbers and the accommodation available. It is little use to canvas the theoretical desirability of two classes when only one class can be formed: the question is, how can that single class best be placed so that it is maximally useful? In general, it is best to have not more than two age groups together, and to place the class as low down in the school as possible. This implies that the children, after spending say their first and second year in the special class, are then absorbed into the ordinary classes, which in their turn have placed on them the onus of providing special educational treatment for those children who need it. It is a good rule to follow that if special help is required it should be given sooner rather than later—in the junior school timely help may be given with reading so that at least some of the children may be 'over the hump' before they are returned to the ordinary class, and in the secondary modern school it may be helpful to keep them with one teacher while they are young and not expose them to a specialist programme until their third year. Of course, the actual numbers in the different age groups and the progress of the 'bulge' will determine where the class can most usefully be placed in a given case, but other things being equal, it is well to place it as low as possible. In any case, in secondary modern schools, the numbers on the roll dwindle as the fourth year proceeds, so there is rarely as acute a pressure at the top as there is at the bottom. The discrepancies in numbers resulting from there being say three classes into which eight-year-olds may go and only two for nine-year-olds, can usually in larger schools be ironed out by adjustments without greatly compromising the principle of confining the special class to a two year range—though an exception may occur in a five class school where there is less leeway for adjustment if the numbers are intractable.

As an actual example, the Head Master of a nine-class junior school organised his classes so that there were two streams, and an extra class containing first and second year children. The extra class contained thirty-two children, so that on an average sixteen children in each year group were getting special help. It is true that this continues for only two years, but at the end of that time many of the children are able to read and can adapt adequately in the ordinary class. If, on the other hand, only six or seven of the intake from the

Infants had entered a seven to eleven special class,[1] there would have been no alternative for the remainder than the crowded IB, less attention, less incentive to master the difficulties of reading, and consequent backwardness. It may be said that this remainder needs special help only temporarily, but if it needs it at the time of its entry into the school, it should have it then, and not be left until some years have passed: in this way, much avoidable backwardness can be prevented. One of the bad consequences of a too narrow conception of special educational treatment in the junior school (criticised earlier as confining special educational treatment to a small handful of markedly aberrant children contrasted with the normal majority who don't need anything) is that the 'normal' children (who may be in fact pretty slow and dull at the bottom of the B stream) are left to sink or swim, and if they sink they become candidates for 'remedial teaching' at a later date, when their difficulties have become ingrained and set by years of—avoidable—failure. This is a thoroughly wasteful procedure, and it is much better to spread the net widely in the early years.

The drawback, of course, is that the children return to the ordinary classes in the third year, even though their need for special educational treatment continues. Of these, an occasional child may be transferred to the E.S.N. school, but there always are children who though not needing to go to the E.S.N. school are not really up to an ordinary class. But still, on balance, I would say that it is a lesser evil that this should happen, since at least the teacher of 3B is made aware of the 'problems' and the need for modifications in their case, than the seven to eleven situation which apparently covers the need and in fact does not. The point is that, whatever way you

[1] Note, too, that while it is desirable for the class to be kept small, it is less essential for it to be *particularly* small than where it caters for a four-year age range of the most difficult children.

stretch it, something has to go, and that in making his choice this way, the Head Master was making the best use of his limited resources. Naturally, it would be nice if he had more resources, but that is another matter.

In general, it may be as well to remind ourselves that ideal solutions are rarely to be found, and that the most practicable organisation is that which provides the widest benefits.

We may conclude that, wherever possible, there should be at least two special classes to cover the four-year age range, and that single classes, as a general rule, are wise to limit their age range to two years and usually to take children from the lower classes of the school. Numerous exceptions to this will occur in practice, but the principle should be clear.

II. TRANSFER CLASSES

Up to the present we have been considering special educational treatment given in the school where the child is already attending, but for a variety of reasons this may not always be provided. The expedient is sometimes adopted of setting up a class or classes in a central conveniently placed school, and drafting in children from other schools for special educational treatment. The classes are variously called special classes, opportunity classes, and the like, but because they have in common the fact that children are transferred from one school to another, and in order to distinguish them from special classes within a single school attended only by pupils of that school, I propose to call them transfer classes. In some cases, they are set up as remedial classes, in others, they are intended for dull and troublesome children, and in still others they contain a mixture of both types.

In so far as such classes are established singly, they fall under the general comments made earlier about single classes, but in addition they raise certain issues of their own.

The first is simply an *a fortiori* argument. If, as was suggested earlier, a single class is likely to be inadequate to meet the needs of even one school, unless it is a small one, how much more inadequate is it when it is considered to be a provision for a group of schools!

One needs to distinguish here between the occasional expedient and a set policy. It is understandable that a local inspector or psychologist likes to have up his sleeve a sympathetic teacher with whom he can place a child whom it is necessary to transfer from his previous school for some good reason. Such emergencies do arise, and means must be found of meeting them. But the situation is quite different if it becomes part of local policy to establish such transfer classes as the Authority's answer to the obligations laid on it under the 1944 Act to provide special educational treatment for those children who need it. Not only does it not cover the need, but it directs attention away from that need. I have given reasons for believing that the more a special class become 'special' in the sense of 'exceptional', the less likely it is to influence the ordinary practices of the school. If it is intended to use successful work in one class as an object lesson for other classes, there must be something in common between their situations. If, for instance, an Authority wishes to improve the standard of C stream teaching, it can best do so by showing a C stream class that is working well, difficulties and all. However excellent the transfer classes, and some of them *are* excellent, they may point a questionable moral if they widen the gap between themselves and the ordinary classes, instead of reducing it. It has been suggested that special educational treatment in the ordinary schools should be thought of in terms of width and suitability of provision, rather than of extra specialness; and that a continuum or spectrum along which children's difficulties in learning can be arranged from greatest to least is a more useful picture for a teacher to have than a block rigidly divided into categories of 'ordinary' and 'special'. A teacher who is already too prone to think in terms of normal and abnormal is more likely to be hindered than helped to form a wider view if his Authority's policy encourages him to think of special educational treatment as the provision of exceptional measures for the exceptional few, and beyond that, no change at the tail end of the streams. As I see it, the place for exceptional measures is in a separate special school, and the characteristic contribution of the ordinary school to special educational treatment should be in width and flexibility, not in narrowness.[1]

Secondly, transfer classes raise certain administrative difficulties. These can be briefly mentioned, for if the principle is a good one, administrative difficulties can be overcome, and if it is not, they are no more than additional arguments against it. The co-operation of parents and teachers is not always easy to ensure: the suspicions of the former and the defensiveness of the latter, both as regards the adequacy of their attempts on a child's behalf and as regards the ticklish matter of total number on roll and the grading of the school, can lead to rear-guard actions, disputes, appeals, and possible delay. From the child's point of view, transfer is likely to be an unsettling experience and may be variously and erroneously interpreted in his phantasy. Transport is sometimes difficult to arrange. Vacancies are not always available when required. It is true that these and similar complications apply also when the transfer of a child to a special school is contemplated, and too much should not be made of them for this reason, but in general it is much easier to explain the transfer of a child from an ordinary to a special school than it is when he is, apparently, just being moved from one ordinary school to another. It must be remembered, too, that single classes are more evanescent

---

[1] Compare, for instance, the statement in Pamphlet No. 30 that special educational treatment is not 'a matter of segregating the seriously handicapped from their fellows but of providing in each case the special help or modifications in regime or education suited to the needs of the individual child' (p. 1).

than special schools: as the teacher moves, even if it is only to another school in the district, the scheme falls down and the children are left high and dry, for the greater the build-up of Mr X's exceptional gifts, the less likely it is that someone can be found to take his place quickly.

The sum of these administrative points adds up to a certain inflexibility in practice: there is likely to be a time-lag while the children are the subject of official deliberation and action, and it is difficult to see how this can be avoided, once administrative machinery has been evoked. The point is, that to provide for children in their own school does not need administrative machinery.

Thirdly, and more seriously, it is not always easy for an Authority to evaluate the success of its transfer classes. The argument goes: 'We cannot make good provision on a wide scale, so we will make provision on a narrow scale and heap this one class with facilities, and then it must be good.' It is the obverse of the quality-quantity distinction which was noted in a previous chapter, and unfortunately it is invalid as an argument. In one case, which I very much hope was exceptional, an Authority established a transfer class and quite properly equipped it generously, put a well-qualified teacher in charge, and made sure that admissions were regulated through the local Child Guidance Clinic. At the time I saw it, it had been going for a year. There were then eight children on the register of whom seven were present, and I can honestly say that nothing was going on which would have been beyond the capacity of a beginning teacher to provide, with forty children to prepare for. In adjoining rooms the usual large classes were to be found. It made one ashamed of the name of special educational treatment.

Enquiries later revealed that the Officers of the Authority had no qualms about the success of the class: they had more than generously done their part and they took it for granted that Mr X, who was considered in the district to be expert with backward children, was also doing his. They were not worried about the small numbers, as they avowedly intended to provide a really high-quality education, and having paid for it, like the Emperor with his new clothes, it was easy to imagine that because the new clothes were expensive they must be good.

It is not intended to suggest that this is anything but a rare result, and it is cited only to show that lavish provision and good provision need not be synonymous. More frequently the difficulty of forming an adequate judgment on the merits of the *principle* stems from the excellence of the example. In most cases, the transfer classes are good and the standard is much higher than in the average run-of-the-mill backward class, as of course it should be. When one considers the advantages with which they start—the *éclat* of a new beginning, the prestige which comes to a class from having the official blessing of the Local Authority, small numbers, good equipment, a teacher who is specially selected for his interest, knowledge, and qualifications—it is not surprising that the classes are successful. It may seem unduly carping in such circumstances to raise a doubt whether the *principle* for which they are such an excellent advertisement is in fact a good one, but the possibility which must be faced is that the success of a transfer class is due not so much to the merits of this type of organisation as to the good teacher and the good conditions. In other words, an Authority cannot always easily evaluate the worth of its transfer classes by a simple comparison with existing ordinary backward classes.

Let us consider what happens when Miss Smith, who has been very successful with 1D in a secondary modern school, is put in charge of a single transfer class. For Miss Smith, the attraction is simple: she feels she has been promoted and that she is recognised as someone very special. The group she now

teaches is much more heterogenous and more obviously difficult, and to compensate for the wide spread of ages she is given
smaller numbers, better equipment, and much more prestige.
The administrator has something he can report to his Committee: a new Opportunity Class has been set up, the office has
done a lot of work in arranging transfers and transport, and
twenty very difficult children are now being well catered for.
What he does not report to his Committee is that thirty merely
difficult children are now being less well catered for: they can
pass from his official purview unless and until some of them
reach the 'very difficult' category. Too much should not be
made of this line of argument: it can be twisted into a reason
for never providing any special facilities at all, and it may very
well be desirable that Miss Smith's special gifts should be exer-
cised on exceptionally difficult children rather than partially
'wasted' on some who might respond to a less able teacher, but
at least it is worth noting that there is another side to the
balance sheet, the loss to the merely difficult ones, and this is
a loss which is not usually presented to the Education Committee. But the really important principle at the back of it is
whether special educational treatment in ordinary schools is
to be narrow or to be wide in scope. In my opinion it would be
a pity if the principle is prejudged because the best teachers of
backward children are chosen for the transfer classes. On a
short run, these classes can show good results as is only to be
expected, but in the long run the implications of their success
may prove to be less wholly satisfactory.

Up to this point in this section the discussion has assumed
the presence of an E.S.N. school in the district, and also that
the ordinary schools from which the transfers are made are
quite large ones. A more difficult position arises when either or
both of these conditions do not apply.

Take first the case of a small school where there is no likelihood that special educational treatment will ever be able to be

provided, and all that can be hoped is that the children's work will be as suitable as possible—the sort of school that is envisaged under paragraph 66 of the Ministry's Pamphlet No. 5. 'An Authority may decide that in the circumstances of a particular school special educational treatment for educationally subnormal children could not be provided there.' As was suggested in the previous chapter, if there are any children from such schools who should be in the E.S.N. school it is particularly important that they should be discovered as soon as possible. There may, however, be others who require special help though not in the E.S.N. school, and in their case it is entirely reasonable for their transfer to another ordinary school to be encouraged. There is, however, a difference between such occasional transfers, and a *policy* of establishing transfer classes even if some of the schools from which the children come are, or could be, able to make their own arrangements. It is the latter which has been criticised here.

The second complication occurs when the area has no E.S.N. school, but is nevertheless fairly well populated (in a really thinly populated rural area the question falls at once, as the suggested movements could never be made to work, and residential provision is the only alternative to the local school). The establishment of a special class may then be advocated, to which can be transferred those children who in a city would be undoubted candidates for a special school. The transfer class then becomes as it were a miniature E.S.N. school—with the crucial disadvantage that it is placed within the framework of an ordinary school. Now this is to make the worst of both worlds. There are advantages in treating all educable children, dull or mentally handicapped, within one flexible plan in, say, a secondary modern school, and there are advantages in removing those most handicapped to an entirely new setting in a special E.S.N. school, but to distinguish them as a separate group while still leaving them within a much larger body is to ask for trouble. Here, again, an occasional transfer in an individual case may be wise, of, for instance, a child attending a very small school, but there is all the difference in the world between this and moving mentally handicapped children irrespective of how well they are being cared for already. Schools A, B and C, for instance, are secondary modern schools within the same town, and School A has a particularly good scheme for backward children which embraces the whole of the D stream—that is, about 100 children, among whom are five mentally handicapped children. The scheme is mooted that School B shall receive all the mentally handicapped children from each school into a single class of about fourteen children, with an age range of eleven to fifteen. Each school will retain its usual streamed organisation, but School B will have its transfer class in addition. This seems unwise, for if it is decided that these children are so deeply handicapped as to need a special environment of their own, away from the D class children with whom they have previously been, then surely they should *be* on their own, not passed on as an excrescence to a school whose main preoccupation must inevitably be its normal majority.

This type of action is sometimes advocated as the first step to the establishment of an E.S.N. school. A number of mentally handicapped children, say of junior age, is gathered together in a transfer class attached to a junior school, and it is hoped gradually to extend it, until it becomes a school of its own. If this be indeed the policy, it would probably be wise to establish it as a separate unit from the beginning, as otherwise awkward questions of jurisdiction are only too likely to arise, between the teacher-in-charge and the Head Master of the parent school. A special school is an entity with its own standards and its own hours: it is differently regarded by the Ministry: its teachers receive additional payment—at what point does the growing fledgling attain this status? and also, when does it move into its own premises? On the one hand, the special school has the advantage that it can devote itself entirely to the task of helping its handicapped children, and in this lies its justification for the segregation it involves: on the other hand, the ordinary school has the advantage that it can deal with a wider range of children, without separating them out: this hybrid would neatly combine the drawbacks of both. If the number of mentally handicapped children in a district is too small for them to form even a small separate school, it is doubtful if transfer classes can become a suitable substitute.

III. THE MULTIPLE APPROACH

The argument of this chapter has been that special educational treatment in ordinary schools, as opposed to special schools, should seek to cover a wide range, and to include a large number of children in its purview. It is easy to criticise the shortcomings of some C and D classes, particularly when they are given few facilities, but at least they cover the ground in a way which one cannot imagine would ever be possible with a network of more sophisticated expedients. When all is said and done, the great majority of backward children do not attend Remedial Centres, or enter a 'single' class, or get a chance to move into a transfer class—but they pursue their inglorious path through the inglorious D stream.

The last type of organisation to be considered is that which accepts the ordinary pattern of streaming and tries to show what can be achieved with it.

Let us suppose the Head of a four stream secondary modern school some years ago to be considering his organisation for the following year. He knows that he has a number of slow and dull children, and he wishes to do justice to them, as he wishes to do justice to all the children in his school. If he were ideally placed with four excellent teachers for four backward classes. he would not need to worry, but then neither would his decision be worth describing. As it is, he has got one very good teacher of backward children, Mr Jones, and he wants to use him to the best advantage. To put Mr Jones with a single special class is tempting, but he rejects it for the following reasons: (1) He would still be left with a number of backward children who would have to go elsewhere. (2) Numbers in each age group would be thrown out. (3) By placing three other teachers in association with Mr Jones, he hopes that Mr Jones' influence and methods will be disseminated over a wider field than if he had been separated from the rest of his colleagues by the boomerang word 'special'. (4) He reflects that over the years, Mr Jones' guidance will reach more boys if he sees a larger number for one year each, than if he sees a small number for four years, and this seems to him preferable. So, Mr Jones becomes the leader of a team of four, with a post of special responsibility for the general oversight of the classes of backward children. It is to be understood that Mr Jones is a teacher of a calibre comparable with those who are selected to take transfer classes, and that he is given reasonably good facilities and the full backing of his Head—only so is it fair to compare the merits of this type of organisation with those of single classes.

It is to be expected that the results in a school with this approach are somewhat uneven, for while Mr Jones' handling of his class may compare in excellence with some of the best single and transfer classes, the other three are unlikely to equal this high standard. Mr Jones, as the leader, has placed himself with the *lowest* of the four classes, ignoring the traditional dictum that the place of honour is with the biggest children (perhaps also to quell the indiscipline that has come as a result of allowing children to proceed up the school with their needs unmet!) Instead, he argues that the youngest class is likely to contain the highest proportion of non-readers and so his technical skill is needed to deal with them. If he can reduce the number of non-readers while the children are with him it will be easier for the next man: then, too, he hopes to set a tone at the beginning which, with luck and the co-operation of his colleagues, may possibly endure. He is not always lucky and his hopes are not always realised, but at least the key to his approach is that he is working with and on other people—'on', because his influence and guidance are available for his less experienced colleagues. They have more motive to consult him than they would have to consult the equally good teacher of a 'single' class, for there his problems would be thought of as different from theirs. He is less a solo star, and more the leader of a team, and if his team is weak, it is his failure as well as theirs. He is able, judiciously, to utilise the varied talents and interests of the members of his team by encouraging them to take a subject in which they are particularly interested with classes other than their own, and in this way he can himself keep in touch with the boys who have passed through his hands and are now in higher classes, and can keep himself aware of their later development. This division is most useful when his colleagues can offer among themselves the subjects which in any case would have to be taken by specialists, e.g. physical education, craft, but nevertheless the amount of specialisation is strictly limited, and the approach of all four classes is pre-dominantly child-centred, not subject-centred. It is sometimes argued that a single class exempted from the specialist round is all that headmasters can be expected to swallow, and the 'special' class is left in splendid isolation in this respect—but surely if the needs of the children are taken into consideration there are a large number who are helped more if their class work is visibly integrated by a single teacher than if it is sub-divided. (In passing, it may be remarked that there is need for a careful rethinking of the whole question of specialisation in secondary modern schools, as it affects the average pupil and certainly as it affects those who are at all backward.) In the case at issue, Mr Jones' headmaster is prepared to cut specialisation to the minimum for these four classes (though, recognising that Mr Jones' three colleagues are not primarily interested in backward children, he wisely lets them recuperate by taking some brighter classes in their favourite subject!) I have gone into some detail on the question of specialisation, as the type of organisation I am describing is to be sharply distinguished from the completely specialist streamed school, where the only difference between the top stream and the bottom is that the former completes the syllabus successfully and the latter does not. We all know the sort of school where the science master complains that the D children cannot even copy off the board, the history master is in despair about their written work and hasn't really comprehended that some in the class cannot read the textbook, much less understand it, and the English is neatly split up so that you go to one specialist for drama, another for poetry, while basic usage is below their notice so that (with the D forms) it is taken by the most junior form master, and some poor unfortunate has 4D for an hour for 'spelling'. There is little to be said for this type of treatment for backward children, and it is understandable that the single class should have revolted against it. It would, however, be a pity if the revolt should stop there and be confined to a single class: what is advocated here is that it should go further and include the whole of the D stream, and perhaps the C stream as well.

As I see it, the single class has the merit of integrating the work and handling of the children, but at the cost of splitting itself off from the rest of the school: what I have called the multiple approach not only preserves this unity of handling, but also, since it caters for a sizeable portion of the school, deals with backwardness as an integral whole. I have seen this approach working over several years in a number of schools, and it is uniformly successful. In one, the leader is also responsible for the selection and allocation of entrants into the different first year classes: in another, where the gap between Mr Jones and his colleagues is less marked, and the ideal of an equal team of keen teachers more nearly approached than in any other school I know, the excellence of the whole scheme for the treatment of backward children received particular commendation after a full inspection of the school: in a third, a very large school of eight streams, the two bottom streams are regarded as a unit for the purpose of providing special educational treatment, i.e. eight classes, or almost a little school in itself. So far, the examples have been taken from secondary modern schools. Junior schools do not have the specialisation difficulty to contend with, but neither do they have the tradition of leadership which goes with departmentalisation, and which enabled Mr Jones to carve out his province, comparable with those of his senior colleagues who were severally responsible for the social studies, the mathematics, and the English of the school. In contrast, there is no difficulty about junior teachers retaining their class, but there is no guarantee that they will follow a common policy in their separate kingdoms. If, however, this difficulty can be overcome by tact and example, it points the way to what seems to be by far the most hopeful approach to backwardness in the Junior School.

Mr Brown was appointed deputy head of a four stream junior school. It was generally understood that he had ideas on the subject of backwardness, but the headmaster was genuinely startled when he asked to be given 1D as his class (he might have been less startled had he been asked to form a brand new single class). There was no difficulty in complying with this request, and he proceeded to do a really solid job. The children were interested, steady, and encouraged to make progress: the backing of the parents was obtained; and gradually the interest of other teachers was caught. This last is the crucial point, for the other results could be expected to follow from any really good work, but only where numbers, conditions and facilities are similar can the other teachers be expected to identify themselves with what is going on. (Of course, it is not as simple as this, and discontent rather than emulation can result, but at least Mr Brown has shown that it can be done and it is for the others to decide whether they mean to follow.) It is undeniable that the Mr Browns are not to be found in every school, but granted his unusual gifts, I would suggest that his Authority is making better use of him where he is, than if he were in charge of a single transfer class. I believe that the core of the whole problem of the adequate treatment of backwardness lies in the junior school, and certainly the most intractable difficulties are to be found there. The only solution that is likely to be effective in the long run, having regard to the size of the problem, must come from some such approach.

If we compare a really good single class with a really good example of a multiple approach (and only this comparison is fair), the thing that stands out is the relative isolation of the former. Mr White in the single class is doing excellent work and visitors remark on his care and effort for the sake of his boys and the unusually good relationship that exists between him and them: within the room he has established a most attractive microcosm. But the trouble is that it stops at the door of the room, and has little carry over to the rest of the school. One of his constant difficulties is that it is hard to move out any children into another class as there is nowhere suitable for them to go.[1] By contrast, Miss Black has no fears on this score, for the work of her class is just one part of a solid unit which is well integrated into the general pattern of the school. If Mr White should leave, his special class (like so many others) will fade away, but Miss Black's departure, though it would

---

[1] It is interesting that since this was written the change which I am advocating is taking place in this school. 'Mr White' is now leading a team at the suggestion of H.M.I.

mean a drop in the *standard,* would not be fatal to the whole *organisation.* The C stream, like the brook, goes on for ever, whether it be good or indifferent, but even if it be indifferent it must be remembered that the children are there and have to be dealt with anyway, and there is always the hope that in the future the standard can be revived to its former excellence. It is the difference between a very beautiful patch which is yet alien to the rest of the educational fabric, and something which is recognisably of the same stuff though better fashioned and sewn.

In the short run, single and transfer classes are likely to achieve striking success, particularly if the best teachers of backward children are encouraged to work in them, but in the long run I cannot see any solution to the problem of special educational treatment in ordinary schools that does not carry the C and D classes—which contain the great mass of backward children—along with them. It may very well be that the conditions are too intractable and the problem insoluble: if so, then to salvage what one can is intelligible. But as long as there is any chance of a solution, it seems better to face the need rather than to run away from it by providing extra special facilities which of their nature could never be made sufficiently widely available. If all the Mr Browns are allowed to show what can be done if they are given reasonably good but by no means super-excellent facilities, that still may not be enough to leaven the lump; but it is a counsel of despair to place them above the battle. It has been repeatedly urged that it is no criticism of a good transfer class that there are not more of them, but it *is* a criticism that not only does it not meet the need, but that it points away from the need into a blind alley. The multiple approach could conceivably be generalised into an all embracing scheme, but of its nature the transfer class is too partial and too limited for generalisation. Instead of emulating the activities of Jack Horner, in their dealing with backward

138

children, Authorities are likely to get further if they encourage the Browns and the Blacks as well as the Whites, and endue their work with an equal prestige.

In this day and age, enough is known of the nature and treatment of backwardness for many people to be acquainted with the sort of approach which is most likely to be successful. We do not need to be told that good teachers in good conditions will achieve good results: that has been often enough shown in the past. But what we most pressingly need to know, is how to apply this recognised experience to what may be called conditions of mass production—the average teachers working in average conditions, and I would suggest that the only final test of special educational treatment in ordinary schools is to be found in their success or failure. When all is said and done, the majority of the backward children come within their care. If they are fortified and supported, even if only a little, more will have been done to help more children, than by partial expedients however excellent they may be.

CHAPTER X

Remedial Measures

ELATIVELY little has been written about remedial measures and what there is, is scattered through educational journals rather than discussed at length.[1] The success of the Remedial Education Centre attached to Birmingham University, and of well-established ventures like that of Burton-on-Trent, has however become widely known, and at the present time many Authorities are discussing or implementing plans for establishing such centres. Remedial Centres are becoming fashionable,[2] but before the momentum becomes irresistible it may be worth while to examine the conditions necessary for their success, the various forms they may take, and the advantages and drawbacks of each.

When Professor Schonell drew attention to the prevalence of preventable backwardness (as distinct from the inevitable

---

[1] *British Journal of Educational Psychology*: June 1950, L. B. Birch, 'The Improvement of Reading Ability'; November 1951, H. B. Valentine, 'Some Results of Remedial Education in a Child Guidance Clinic'; February 1954, W. Curr and N. Gourlay, 'Experimental Evaluation of Remedial Education'; November 1953, M. L. Kellmer and R. Gulliford, 'A Note on Experimental Evaluation of Remedial Education'.

Educational Review of the Birmingham Institute of Education, vol. VI, Nos. 1, 2 and 3 (1953-4). J. E. Collins, 'Remedial Educational Provision for children of average or above-average intelligence'.

[2] The quantity and variety of schemes outlined in Collins' articles are extremely impressive. His information, however, was obtained by replies to a postal questionnaire and in such circumstances it is not always easy to evaluate the worth of the undertaking; thus side by side with one scheme which I know to be well-founded and careful he mentions another which also I know and is merely (rather bad) coaching.

backwardness which results from innate dullness) he advocated serious and organised attempts to provide remedial instruction for those children whose attainments in one or more of the tool subjects were seriously behind their own potential. They might be generally retarded in all their work, or they might be working up to capacity with the exception of one or two subjects in which they had a specific difficulty. He defined children with a specific difficulty as being those 'whose ability in a subject . . . was at least 1½ years below their other educational attainments and general intellectual level'.[1] Retardation can thus apply to children of all levels of intelligence, the bright as well as the dull. Sporadic attempts to help such retarded children to catch up, for instance after absence, are of course common in schools, and they attain varying degrees of success. There is no doubt that prompt first aid of this kind by the teacher who knows the child is the first line of defence. The difficulty comes when either such first aid is not given or is not successful. We then have a situation which all too often progressively worsens as the child becomes older, increasingly confused, and apathetic or troublesome. It would appear only common sense to have *organised* arrangements whereby such children can be helped before the situation gets too much out of hand. Still at the common sense level, it would appear evident that quite large numbers of children will need to be provided for. Yet in fact children usually reach the remedial teacher only when their difficulties are well marked, and time-consuming to remedy. Evidently few children will be helped in this way. We seem to be chasing a contradiction here between a widely felt need and a narrowly applied solution, between fairly large minorities that are candidates for help and the small numbers and necessarily restricted case load of the remedial teachers, between in fact preventive and remedial work. There would appear to be an analogy with the treatment of innately dull pupils. Just as a special E.S.N.

[1] *Backwardness in the Basic Subjects*, p. 80.

school to cater for the markedly handicapped does not obviate the provision on a much wider scale of arrangements for dull pupils in ordinary schools; so the need for a special centre for remedial treatment should be considered *together with* widespread preventive measures.

It is worth while to start off by putting remedial work in its context of prevention, as otherwise there would be little defence against the cynic who defines remedial measures as locking the stable door after the horse has gone'. From this point of view, the value of a Remedial Centre should be judged not merely in terms of its success with its own clients, who form a small and highly selected minority, but by the extent to which its efforts are reflected in the schools of its area. Birch, writing of the Burton centre, pointed out that a considerable decline in reading retardation throughout the borough was evident after the centre had been established for two years, and he attributed this to the fact that the class teachers had become 'reading conscious'. Critics who challenge his conclusions may point out that *post hoc* is not necessarily *propter hoc,* and that some of the improvement may be spontaneous recovery after the dislocations caused by the war years (his observations were made between 1947 and 1949), but the point we are concerned with is the entire propriety of his attempt to link efforts in the Centre with conditions in the schools. Authorities where large classes in the primary schools are the rule need not be surprised if much preventable backwardness results; and it is arguable that an even spread of available teachers is more efficient than withdrawing some of them to cope, belatedly, with the deficiencies traceable to over-large classes at an earlier stage. It is true that small classes are not a universal panacea, but neither, emphatically, is the setting up of *ad hoc* schemes for coping with backwardness if more efficient arrangements in the original place of instruction—the school—would have sufficed. Remedial centres, then, far from being a goal in themselves, are the sign of an imperfect state of affairs. They exist to help children from the schools, but not in isolation from the schools. There is no virtue in an elaborate organisation if a simpler one would work, and first attention should go to helping children, if possible, within their own schools. But it is not always possible, and the effective choice is sometimes between failing with a particular child and attendance at the remedial centre, and in that case there is no doubt where the choice would lie. There is, however, a world of difference between this conception of remedial centres as a residual service, a last line of defence, and as the complete answer to problems of retardation, while leaving the schools untouched. In my opinion, the latter would be a very shortsighted policy. It is spectacular to establish a network of centres, but unless something is done at the same time to cut at the sources of supply, little of value results, and the problem is simply perpetuated. It should therefore be axiomatic that when a centre is set up, liaison between it and the schools it serves should be considered extremely important.

We pass now to consider the various forms the centre may take. It may be a place where the children attend full-time (to become, in effect, a special school or class): or, more commonly, a place where children go for one or more sessions a week, while remaining on the roll of their own school. Each method has characteristic advantages and drawbacks.

The big advantage of the full-time method is that the child can be known and educated as a whole person. His reading disability (or whatever it was that occasioned his transfer) does not occupy the entire picture, but takes its place as part only (admittedly an important part) of his education. Coaching that degenerates into cramming is thus avoided, for the mechanics of reading can be learnt, as they should be and as they normally are by the averagely successful child, as part of an all round scheme of instruction which takes in all elements of the curriculum. Again, the effects of his disability on him as a person can be noted and minimised. At a time when we all pay lip-service to the emotional concomitants of backwardness, it seems odd that our efforts should so often take the form of a direct attack on the presenting symptom. This is perhaps all that can be done when time is limited, but one of the advantages of the full-time school or class is that a wider viewpoint can be taken, and attention properly paid to his emotional and social development, as well as to instruction in reading. Finally, there is some advantage in removing a seriously retarded child entirely from the competitive struggle of an ordinary classroom, rather than expecting him to cope with it part-time. At the same time, the full-time class has corresponding drawbacks. Take first the question of stigma. Parents are prone to confuse this transfer with transfer to a special E.S.N. school, and even if their misunderstandings can be cleared up, those of neighbours and other children remain. It can be argued that if the child's need is great enough, this consideration is unimportant, but even so it can cause trouble: it is therefore desirable that attention be paid to public relations, so that parents and teachers are made aware of the true functions of the Centre. A more important difficulty is the double break in continuity, when the child is transferred to the centre, and when he returns to his ordinary school. Everyone would agree that such transfers should be avoided if possible—another argument for helping children within their own school—but if he is not profiting in the slightest there does come a point where on balance it seems the lesser evil to give him a chance elsewhere, until he *is* able to cope with his ordinary school. So far, the drawbacks considered have been external to the centre, but there are further difficulties within the centre itself. A full-time centre is extremely hard to organise. By definition, the difficulties it deals with are remediable, and as they are remedied the children depart: the population is therefore shifting. Enough children to fill even a small school cannot be gathered together except in large urban areas, and transport difficulties may result. But on the other hand, a unit of one or two classes is liable to contain wide variations in age, mental age, and social maturity, and provides considerable problems for the teachers. Then there is the question of equipment and facilities for practical work, particularly for senior children. To transfer a boy who is keen on woodwork and relatively good at it from a well equipped modern school to a small unit with few facilities may result in antagonising him rather than in gaining his interest and co-operation. (Too much should not be made of this objection, but neither should it be ignored.) Perhaps the unit is attached to an existing school, and shares its facilities. Then difficulties may arise over jurisdiction, discipline (particularly if the parent school has not been well chosen, and wide discrepancies of conception exist), status, or comparisons (which may be odious) between the unit and the parent school in such things as size of class, attainments, or allowance for expendable stock. No scheme works better than the people who are involved in it, and though these difficulties may sound carping and petti-fogging, they can be very real in practice, for teachers after all are human, and if there is continual friction the children will not benefit, however ideal the scheme sounds on paper. Then, too, it is not only the teachers who may find co-operation difficult: a more common source of trouble is in children's comments, which are hard to check. Whatever the difficulties involved in special educational treatment for backward or retarded children within a single school, those difficulties are intensified (as was pointed out in the previous chapter) when the unit is known to be separate and yet is within the school. Devices such as separate playtimes increase the sense of being different and the likelihood of derogatory comment when, as is inevitable, the children must at some time meet. If one alleged reason for siting the unit within an existing school is to give the children the advantages of wider social contacts than they would get in their small group, it seems an odd way of doing it, and might easily create more problems than it solves. It seems fair to conclude that the game is not worth the candle, and that if a separate unit is to be envisaged, it should have its own premises. Granted that exceptional people can make almost any arrangement work, it does seem safer in considering the pros and cons of suggested organisations to avoid those that seem unnecessarily productive of tensions. Assuming, then, that the unit has its own premises, the difficulties, both social and educational, of an unusually small group remain. Are the seniors to go to the nearest school for practical subjects and games, or are they to miss these elements of a balanced education? John is big and strong and cock of the walk too easily: it so happens that Jane is the only girl of her age and is becoming lonely and shut in: the tone of the group as a whole is more swayed, for good or ill, by one or two individuals than would be a larger unit. It is true that these remarks apply equally to any small unit anywhere (e.g. in a village school) and they can be utilised constructively as well as destructively, but the special point here is that by hypothesis they occur in a large urban area where the usual social and educational pattern is quite different. Whatever answer to the question whether this is a good or bad departure from the norm is given, it is at least important that the query should be asked, before setting up arrangements without considering their implications for the whole school life of the children concerned. If it is claimed as an advantage for the full-time centre that it can attend to the children's emotional and social development, it must equally be admitted that the actual influences on the children should be taken into account. Similar considerations apply to the schoolwork of the children. Older children, many of whom are of good or average intelligence, require an outlet for their widening interests in the world around. They *may* be backward in reading, or in arithmetic, but the tasks they are given, in social studies, in general science, in local surveys, should be commensurate with their age and intelligence (though the form in which their work is expressed may need to be scaled down to fit in with their disability in reading). The demands on the teacher are correspondingly great. I once saw a fourteen-year-old boy, of superior intelligence (though very backward) in a special unit, given a task which might have occupied an average nine-year-old for five minutes. With the aid of a small-scale map of the British Isles, he traced the railway route from London to Perth and wrote down the names of the few towns that appeared on the map. No reason was given for the assignment and it did not seem to be connected with anything else. (As the group was very small, the teacher could hardly plead pressure of work.) This seems to me a travesty of special education, and it did not surprise me that under this regime he remained backward and apathetic! It should be remembered that the advantage of the full-time unit lies in its power to harness the children's general interests in the service of improving whatever the disability may be, so that, for instance, his desire to know more in his chosen field may lead him to try to *read* about it. If the standard in general subjects is low, a powerful tool is being neglected. Finally, in the tool subjects themselves, genuine difficulties of organisation abound. The children are all at different levels, their strengths and weaknesses vary from child to child, and individual work is essential. This point will be taken up and extended later, as it is common too to the part-time remedial centre and so it will simply be mentioned here.

Finally, in practice it is found that there are some children who do not make progress. If after ample time has been allowed they show no signs of improving, should they be retained, to the exclusion of another child who might benefit more, or should they return to the ordinary school? This is not an easy question to answer, but it is one which must be faced in considering policy.

To summarise, the full-time remedial centre contains many elements of genuine difficulty, and calls for teachers of considerable skill and persistence.

I would like to end this section with an example where the difficulties are being surmounted. The Centre has its own premises and takes children of junior age (eight to twelve) only: it thus avoids the difficulties of providing for the specialised interests of seniors and at the same time attempts to remedy the retardation as early as possible. With sixty children on roll, and four classes, it avoids the worst organisational difficulties of the very small unit, and so its organisation can be like that of many another small school, with the vital exception that all work in the basic subjects is individual. Children usually stay for one year, and then have improved sufficiently in attainments, attitude to work, and (often) behaviour to return to their original school: it is particularly important to note that although they express reluctance to leave, they nonetheless settle down happily and make satisfactory progress when back in their old school. Some have returned in less than a year, and a few have been kept for more than the year, but only in unusual circumstances. There appears to be a very good relationship both with parents and with the Heads of the local primary schools, once the function of the Centre had been clearly understood and misapprehensions cleared away: and there is close liaison with the local child guidance clinic.

We turn now to the part-time Centre, where the child remains on the roll of his ordinary school, but is absent at stated times, usually once or twice a week, as if he were attending a clinic. (In fact, in the U.S.A. the phrase 'reading clinic' is in common use.) The teacher works with a different group each session for perhaps eight sessions a week: the remaining time, when he is not scheduled to teach, is devoted to recording, the making of apparatus, home and school visits, Child Guidance or Care Committee case conferences and so on. In this way it is claimed that a large number of children can receive skilled help, while still keeping the groups small. Although this method involves certain difficulties of organisation, mainly in connection with journeys of children to the centre, and with fitting an individual into a suitable group when he arrives, the difficulties are not so grave as with a full-time centre, possibly because it claims less. The part-time Centre can leave the all-round education of the children to the ordinary school and become simply a 'reading clinic'—and in this lies its strength and its danger. It has the advantage of a clearly conceived and limited aim, but it is open to the grave disadvantage that it may set its sights too narrowly, and think of its task simply as improving the mechanics of reading or number, apart from the manifold activities of an ordinary school day. There is risk of a schism between the work of the ordinary school (much of which, it should be remembered, has a bearing on the tool subjects) and the work of the centre. Indeed, if the remedial teacher seriously attempted to link the work of his group of six or eight children with the work of the schools from which the children came, he would find himself torn in six or eight different directions: it just cannot be done. But that it is impossible to avoid the risk of confusion in the children's minds is itself a most important fact which must be weighed in the balance against all the advantages which are claimed to follow from sending a child to the centre. In the short run, and as an emergency measure, a boy who cannot be helped at all in his own school may benefit if a centre is set up, but in the long run, before the *policy* becomes established it is necessary to consider carefully this inescapable concomitant. A further concomitant which needs to be taken into account is the effect on the school, and on the conception which it holds of its responsibility to the children in its charge. Anything which might possibly weaken this sense of competence and responsibility should be scrutinised with care. It is true that this argument could be twisted to prevent developments which are undoubtedly beneficial—we do not usually think of school clinics, or speech therapy, as unduly limiting the teacher's responsibility. But possibly a distinction can be drawn here between activities which are peripheral to the teacher's function and those which are central. A good teacher will keep an eye on the physical health of his pupils, but he is relieved when the school nurse is available; he will try to help a boy with poor speech, but he has neither the time nor the technical skill to deal with serious aberrations of speech. Yet it may be said that to apply the same line to classwork (which depends on adequate attainment in the three R's) would be to cut at a matter which is very properly the responsibility of the teacher. This argument is possibly of less weight where specialist teachers in a secondary modern school are concerned: they would say that the last thing they wanted to do was to impart the rudiments of the three R's! But with teachers of younger children, the matter is different. Do we really wish, as a set policy and over a period of time, to encourage the thought 'Children who are failing to work to capacity should attend a remedial centre for specialist attention. But there is no remedial centre in this district (or, alternatively, there is one but the waiting list is very long) so what can I do? I am afraid that I might do the wrong thing and make matters worse.' The point I am trying to make is that, while on the one hand the centre can act as a stimulant and a challenge to some teachers to improve their practices, on the other hand it can cut at the confidence of other teachers in their ability to deal adequately with children of low attainment.

It should be noted that this criticism is more important with a part-time Centre than with a full-time one. Once the decision has been made to transfer John to the latter, he ceases to attend his previous school, as with any other transfer, and therefore the sense of responsibility of the teachers is not damaged as it might be in the case we are discussing.

From all this, it follows that it is vitally important to keep the class teacher in the picture and not to convey, directly or by implication, the impression that his functions have been abrogated. The class teacher will wish to know about the progress of the child, and in particular he will wish to know what steps he can take and what methods he can use without cutting across what the Centre does. A remedial Centre is successful to the extent that it works in co-operation with the school and not in isolation: but, as we said earlier, this is not easy when a number of different schools are concerned.

For this reason, school visits are to be encouraged. Yet these too have their own difficulties. The remedial teacher who goes to confer with the class teacher goes either as an equal, or as an expert, and either way there are pitfalls in their relationship. With skill and tact these can be avoided, and certainly one would not wish to give the impression that ordinary human contacts are so very difficult to establish and maintain, but it would be foolish to overlook the possibility of difficulties arising. (Note again that the visit of the school nurse or the speech therapist is not thought of as a threat to the teacher in the same way.) If he avoids the class teacher and sees only the Head, he suggests the remoteness of a superior being, aloof from the hurly-burly of class conditions. Too frequently the defence of the class teacher is to recall the differences in the size of the groups with which each has to deal. This is not entirely fair, and he probably overlooks the genuine difficulties of the remedial teacher's task, but it is all too human a reaction. Skill in establishing and maintaining good relationships with adults as well as with children is therefore an essential prerequisite of the remedial teacher, and it is one which it is not easy to fulfil. I think it is a fair comment that those who take up this work often are of a highly original and creative turn of mind, but such individualists, however excellent they may be with children, are not always equally successful with adults. Where this is so, the effectiveness of their work is lessened, and the children, as always, are the real sufferers when friction develops between their respective mentors. The full-time Centre *can* exist in splendid but stultifying isolation: the part-time one cannot, and this is both its great opportunity and an additional source of difficulty. Good public relations are essential: and the remedial teacher, even though he walks as delicately as Agag, cannot always escape Agag's fate.

After all this, mere difficulties of organisation within the Centre seem small beer. Yet it is no easy task to make groupings which fulfil the needs of the children adequately, and which provide harmonious social as well as fairly homogeneous educational groups. Then, too, what is meant by homogeneous? The members of a group which is homogeneous in initial level may differ considerably in the methods which help them most, or in rate of progress: they may be slowed up by inter-personal rivalries. It is worth noting that such tensions are often greater in a small group than in the relative impersonality of a large class, particularly when they consist by hypothesis of children who are somewhat insecure and are struggling for recognition. The question of relationship with an adult also needs attention. A group even of three children is still a group: it differs more from an individual pupil-master relationship than it does from a much larger group. The insecure child who must have *undivided* attention is helped less by moving him from a large class to a group of six or eight than one might suppose: indeed rivalries and tensions may even be intensified in the smaller unit, particularly if his difficulties of learning stem, as they often do, from trouble at home. Whereas a school, with its larger pool of available companions and its majority of 'ordinary' children who are easily adaptable, can leave these things to sort themselves out to a considerable extent, they need to be explicitly taken into consideration in a remedial group. Often there is no easy answer, yet if one cannot be found, the overall effect on the children may not be what we imagine it to be. All this is simply to say that we cannot project children into a situation *just* to improve their reading or their arithmetic without its having other repercussions: these implications need to be carefully considered and the experience which the children are receiving thought of as a whole.

A further comment which fits in with the foregoing is that often more is at stake than the mere backwardness in reading or number. Frequently, children who are retarded are first and foremost problem children, and the backwardness is simply a sign of a more deep-seated maladjustment. In such cases a purely educational approach is of little avail, and it is desirable for facilities for Child Guidance examination and treatment to be available. In many areas, selection for the remedial centre is done through the Child Guidance Clinic and where this is so, the problem presumably takes care of itself, but under other circumstances it would need careful watching. In any case, the whole question of selection needs ventilation: it needs to be in the hands of persons who can distinguish adequately between backwardness and retardation, and send to the centre only those children who could and should be doing better than they are.

But perhaps the most important aspect of selection is in choosing the teachers. Remedial work can be either the cushiest job on earth, or one of the most difficult and exacting. It is unfortunate that on a superficial view it might appear the former, as that could attract a flow of applicants of the wrong type. A group of eight children instead of forty appears an attractive proposition: the repetitive arrangements of different groups misleadingly suggests that the afternoon can be similar to the morning and tomorrow to today, instead of preparing seven

L

or eight different lessons for each day: the lure of relative independence beckons those who dislike routine grind, or find it hard to fit in with others, or think they are a cut above the rest and want to be different. In sober fact, the demands on the remedial teacher's patience, adaptability and skill are heavy—I sometimes think, heavier than should be asked of any one person continuously and over a long period of time. It is no good having one pet scheme to which all the children must conform, but *genuine* individual work (as distinct from merely occupying the children) is no joke to prepare and organise for constantly changing groups. He must have high standards for himself and for the children, and be able to maintain those standards in relative isolation, apart from the stimulus to effort which the busy life of a school provides, but at the same time he must not be so dependent for his self-esteem on 'results' that he over-presses the children. He should avoid mumbo-jumbo and the glorification of his work into an esoteric mystery, while at the same time he really must know more than the average teacher about how and why children learn to read, where and why they encounter difficulty, and how these difficulties can be overcome: in fact, the very reverse of the emperor's new clothes. There is no letting-up and no chance for relaxation, and when at last success is achieved and the children are 'over the hump' they cease to attend, and their places are taken by others. The ordinary good teacher who takes an interest in his children after they have left his class, can see them round the school for a year or two and note their progress with pleasure, but this satisfaction is not always open to the remedial teacher. On all these counts, the danger of loss of freshness and deterioration into a routine rule-of-thumb, far from being less in a remedial centre than in a school, seems to me greater: and once this deterioration has taken place, the whole justification for the remedial centre has gone. Remedial work should be done excellently, or not at all.

This may seem an unduly pessimistic review, but it must be remembered that, whatever the faults of schools, they have stood up as institutions for a number of years. An innovation may seem excellent for a short period and in a limited context; but its general adoption should be preceded by careful consideration of its implications both for the children whom it is intended to help and for the teachers who must implement it.

So far the discussion has covered cases in which children are removed from their ordinary premises, but now it is necessary to consider whether they can be given help within the walls of their own school.

The commonest and simplest methods are those where the school makes its own arrangements for helping those who have fallen behind. The Head may take a group of backward readers, or where the school has a floating teacher her services can be utilised, or a supernumerary may attend for part of each day. It is easy to criticise the adequacy of these arrangements, and the lack of skill with which they are sometimes conducted, but their great merit lies in their flexibility and informality and in the speed with which they can be applied. Long before the machinery of an elaborate scheme involving outside experts and careful selection precedures can be put into motion, something is being done, and it will be a bad day when the time comes, if it ever does, that these efforts stop. That is what was meant earlier about cutting at the feeling of the responsibility of the school for its own members. It is a fair criticism that the rule-of-thumb methods by which the children are chosen for these groups tend to overweight them with slow and dull children to the neglect of children who are retarded in that their attainments are passable, but still below their ability, but so far as they go, they are to be welcomed. Whatever their limitations, they do something, and they do it without undue delay and they cover in total a large number of children. It is worth reminding ourselves that numerically this informal first aid covers many more children than any other device, and on this ground alone it is of considerable importance.

Another common solution is for retarded children to be grouped in special 'opportunity' classes. Many of the issues here have already been dealt with, so the discussion can be brief, in so far as it concerns *retarded* children. These classes are either recruited from a pool of schools, or draw their members from one school alone. If the former, they are open to the general comments given earlier about the pros and cons of moving children from school to school. If the latter, the probability is that the so-called 'opportunity' class will in fact contain children of two widely separated types; the innately dull on the one hand, and the retarded on the other. These latter may be of any intelligence level from low to high, and the unfortunate teacher may find herself confronted with an extremely difficult and heterogeneous collection of children, whose needs diverge at every turn. A dull child needs steady practice with a slowly increasing degree of difficulty and limited objectives: a bright but retarded child may start off with equally simple material until he has gained confidence but thereafter he can move more rapidly with a steeper gradient of difficulty and more stimulation. It is not easy to do justice to both groups within the same class, particularly as social difficulties are often added to the educational ones, and the readier-tongued brighter children, however backward they may be from a school point of view, are often quick enough to perceive the limitations of their fellows.

An opportunity class which consisted of retarded children only, would not be open to this objection, but the school would have to be a very large one to provide sufficient retarded children from among its members. Perhaps a more useful expedient than a class in such a very large school might be to arrange remedial groups, on the lines of the Centres previously discussed, but catering only for children from the one school.

These groups would meet for a short period every day, and the rest of the time would be spent in the usual classes. Comprehensive schools might usefully provide facilities for such remedial work, and they would be able to avoid most of the difficulties mentioned earlier. A teacher who was engaged part-time in class teaching and part-time with remedial groups could use each as relief from the other. The dangers of staleness and of over-concentration would be mitigated, and he would have the incentive of watching the continued progress of his 'remedial' children after they had left his care. An immensely valuable sideline would be the effective interplay between the teacher and his colleagues, an interplay which is so much harder to achieve for the remedial teacher who is an outsider and is seen only occasionally, and in any case without his materials and apparatus. To drop into a room just along the corridor from one's own to see what materials Miss A is using and how she goes about it is much easier and more effective than to go by invitation to a centre at some distance to see what one feels may be a put-on exhibition. In this way the fertilising influence of a really good remedial teacher may be felt more strongly than could ever be the case were she working in isolation. Differences of approach can be discussed on the spot, and misunderstandings obviated. It seems to me that there is considerable scope for experiment in remedial groups in large secondary modern and comprehensive schools. Where it is provided as part of the ordinary internal workings of the school, many of the difficulties and objections mentioned earlier would no longer apply.

It is obvious, however, that this expedient would apply only in really big schools where numbers are great enough to occupy a skilled teacher for say half of his time. The final suggestion to be discussed concerns the use of a peripatetic remedial teacher among a number of smaller schools. For the suggestion, it is argued that more effective use can be made of a skilled person by dividing his services among a number of schools than by employing him full-time in one school where inevitably he would spend most of his time on other duties. (The assumption here that such diversion is undesirable could I think be challenged, but let it pass for the time being.) The first question that needs to be asked is: would his function be that of an organiser or of a teacher? If an organiser, helping and advising the teachers who are actually working with the children, valuable as his suggestions might be, there would still be need to define his position *vis-a-vis* not only the teachers, but the Heads, and there might be possibilities of friction and misunderstanding. If he were used in each school actually to teach the children, there is less likelihood of misunderstanding, but more of overworking him. Materials and apparatus would need to be duplicated in each of his schools, and by the nature of things his time in each would be limited, and so the possibility of alternating with a different kind of teaching and thus giving him relief would be remote. At the same time it is fair to say that the graver disadvantages of isolation would be avoided, while the full benefits of dovetailing his activities with those of the other teachers would be lost, for it is difficult to work in a school without belonging to it. It seems that this would be a halfway house between the separate centre and the plan here advocated of integrating remedial work into the ordinary pattern of one school. A more useful compromise might be to challenge the assumption that the most efficient use of his time was to divide him up between a number of different schools, and to argue that while only the largest of schools could employ a man as much as half-time on remedial work, yet a full-time appointment in a moderate-sized school could be justified if the major part of his time was spent, say, in working with the C streams on the lines advocated earlier, together with a small amount of remedial work. In that case, the same teacher would be responsible for work both with the dull and with the retarded within the one school, rather than splitting it vertically and having one arrangement (shared with other schools) for retarded children, and another totally different scheme for the C and D streams. This seems to be a neater and more easily workable plan.

To summarise, in the short run there may be need for remedial centres to deal with the backlog of children whose educational difficulties have accumulated for years, but a more hopeful long-term programme would be to improve facilities within the schools themselves, so that some difficulties are prevented altogether, and the others that arise can be dealt with more quickly. It must be remembered also that though improved *educational* measures can prevent much of the retardation, some of it is a hard-core manifestation of emotional maladjustment, needing much more radical treatment. By 'improving facilities' therefore I mean not only smaller classes, but arrangements for in-service training with a view to helping those Head Teachers who have the responsibility of arranging those informal groupings which I called first aid, and also closer liaison with the Child Guidance Clinics. Authorities which worked on those lines would have little that was spectacular to show, but the results might none the less be sound.

CHAPTER XI

A Note on the Training of Teachers

No schemes, however excellent, work by themselves, and their effectiveness in practice depends on the quality of the people who carry them out. To provide an education suited to the age, aptitude and ability of every child is a stirring idea, but it can be translated into reality only by the teachers. Backward children, even more than others, depend on their teachers for help and guidance, and form a challenge to their skill and ingenuity, for while an average or bright child can make progress even if the quality of the teaching he receives is not very good, a dull child is more likely to be bogged down in his own incomprehension unless his teacher can rescue him. This means that the technical equipment of the teacher must be sound, for example with regard to the teaching of reading. But in the first instance the dull child is likely to be taught by a teacher who is in no sense a specialist in the handling of backward children, but who simply has a number of backward children in his class. The first line of defence, then, is in the ordinary class teacher and in the equipment which he receives in his initial training; and only later does more specialised training fall to be considered.

Initial Training. A very common complaint of some Head Teachers is that their assistants, unless they were trained for infants, have no idea how to teach the basic subjects and in particular the early stages of reading. Several factors have combined in recent years to intensify this complaint. One is the increasing tendency of women's colleges to provide separate courses for nursery teachers, infant teachers, infant-junior teachers, junior teachers, and secondary modern teachers, whereas the smaller colleges of the past provided perhaps only two courses, with an overlap in the middle, one taking the years from five to eleven, and the other the years from nine to fourteen. Although the students are expected to learn about age groups other than their own, and how their chosen age group fits into the general pattern of child development, there may be rather a temptation for a student to consider herself a teacher of 'older juniors', or even of 'nine-year-olds'—nothing more and nothing less. Similarly with the men's colleges except that they always tended to emphasise work with older children. The difficulty came when the students left college, and many of them perforce had to be given classes of an age other than those for which they were trained. Especially in the years after the war, when the 'bulge' came into the infant schools, the demand was particularly for more and more infant teachers, and so the displacement was usually a downward one. This meant that many young teachers, both men and women, were being given classes of children younger than they had bargained, or indeed trained, for, and difficulties in the teaching of reading became especially evident. To some extent the passage of time will ease this particular difficulty, as the 'bulge' moves up the schools and the demand becomes more for teachers of older children—it is often felt that it is easier for teachers to move up than to move down—but there are always likely to be *some* teachers who are displaced and at a loss.

Secondly, there is often some confusion in students' minds between teaching and learning. At a time when emphasis is placed in the colleges on the need for the child to wish actively to learn, the part of the teacher in providing the conditions within which the child can make progress is sometimes underestimated, and a student may interpret 'don't cram' as meaning 'don't teach'. He may think that since a child learns at his own pace and in his own time, it is unnecessary to teach him, as he will 'pick it up' (blessed phrase) when he is ready for it. Now certainly the importance of motivation in learning to read is great, as is evidenced by striking results reported of children in camps and boarding schools when they *need* to read their parents' letters, but it is not the only factor. After all, reading is an artificial activity in a sense in which climbing and jumping are not, and maturation alone cannot give a child a key to the conventional meaning of black marks on paper: he needs also properly graded experiences of the meaning of these symbols, and it is part of the teacher's skill to provide these experiences in an orderly and controlled sequence. If the teacher does not do this, either because he does not know how to, or because he thinks it is 'wrong' to teach, many children will nevertheless succeed in 'picking it up', but others will be more backward than they need have been.

Thirdly, the postponement of formal instruction until children are sufficiently mature means that reading is no longer expected to be completed and done with before the children leave the infant school. Junior Head Teachers find that a sizeable minority of children now come to them unable to read, and while their subsequent progress may well be all the faster because they have not been pushed and chivvied into 'barking at print' before they were ready for it, this is only so provided that the junior teachers are willing and able to teach them. There is therefore a much greater need than there was formerly for junior teachers to be able to teach reading and this need is not confined to those who work with backward classes.

Fourthly, reorganisation has brought together into the secondary modern schools large numbers of children, some of whom are bound to be backward, and at the same time cut them off, so to speak, from their hinterland. In an all-age school the men and women who taught the older children might overlook one or two who could barely read, but if they did not, there were teachers available in the lower classes to whom recourse could be made: the traditional belief that the teaching of reading was an infant teacher's job, or a woman's job rather than a man's, need not be questioned. But now, secondary modern teachers, both men and women, find that this comfortable assumption no longer holds. On the whole, the men are in a more difficult position than the women, for a woman. even if she trained only for seniors, is likely to have seen something of the activities of the other students in her college who were training for infants; the feeling that teaching reading is a task for women dies hard; and backwardness in reading is in any case commoner among boys than among girls. For all these reasons, the Heads of boys' schools are particularly anxious about the position, and men's colleges are now beginning to alter their traditional attitude to the teaching of reading.

There is therefore much to be said for the introduction into the initial period of training of a general course in methods of teaching reading, certainly for all who intend to be teachers of juniors and advisably for secondary modern teachers also,[1] for even those with a strong specialist subject have often to do some form teaching as well and in any case there is no guarantee that they will not at some time need to teach younger children. The course need not be detailed, but it should include some practical experience in the making and use of apparatus, acquaintance with the general principles of the main recognised approaches, and knowledge of some commonly used reading series, together with the teacher's handbooks that go with them. It is preferable that it should be approached by way of the younger normal child, rather than

[1] 'It is suggested that all who will be likely to teach in junior or secondary modern schools should have some acquaintance with methods used for teaching the beginnings of reading, and with the kind of modification necessary for adapting the methods for older pupils.' Ministry of Education Pamphlet No. 18, *Reading Ability*, p. 26.

by way of the backward older one, whose position is often complicated and criss-crossed by additional difficulties. Even though the latter may seem easier to introduce as being nearer to the students' avowed interest in older children, the additional difficulties cannot properly be tackled on account of the students' own inexperience and lack of comparative standards, and for that reason are best avoided. If in his later experience he needs to adapt the methods he has met to the requirements of older children, he is more likely to make the adaptation successfully when he really has a particular group in mind whose needs he knows, than if he tries to do it all in one go at the training college stage, when his knowledge of the children's needs is purely hypothetical. For similar reasons the books recommended should be general rather than detailed—for example, Schonell's *Psychology and Teaching of Reading*, rather than his *Backwardness in the Basic Subjects*. One can sometimes see young teachers struggling with the intricacies of a full scale diagnosis, the details of which are completely beyond them, when what the majority of the children want is some straightforward help and a reading book that is easy enough for them. (These remarks do not suffice, of course, for the minority of really difficult children, nor for the minority of teachers who wish to make helping them their main preoccupation.) In general, it is a good rule that the simplest methods should be tried first, and only if these fail, to invoke more complicated procedures. But it is one thing for a teacher, faced with an actual case of a child or children in whom he has become interested, to set himself to learn what other more specialised procedures are available, and it is quite another if a group of students are simply thrown into the deep end with no means of distinguishing what are the common and what are the much rarer causes of difficulty. In other words, the basic course should be on 'How Children Learn to Read', and not on 'Backward Readers', which is quite a different matter.

It is sometimes possible for training college students to take a small group of children for practice in reading, and to give simple coaching. In doing this they help the children and the teacher, and gain useful experience themselves. The condition of success is, that it should be kept at a simple level, and not allowed to be inflated into something much more pretentious, either in the minds of the students or in those who organise the programme. It is misleading to describe it as 'remedial reading', or as 'diagnostic teaching' when in fact it is just plain coaching, and not very skilled coaching at that.[1] This is not to say that it may not be quite useful within its limits, as long as all concerned are quite clear as to what these limits are.

I have dealt at length with the example of the teaching of reading, as it is a key subject, and it is usually the one chiefly involved when Head Teachers comment on the shortcomings of their new assistants, but similar remarks apply to the teacher's equipment in basic arithmetic. Turning now from the technical armoury of the teacher to his general orientation, as it is dealt with in psychology lectures, I would say that it is much more important for him to have a firm framework of ordinary child development than to go into detail over extreme deviations. If the main emphasis is placed on the surprisingly wide range of behaviour and interests that is compatible with normal development, and if backwardness is treated as a natural and necessary concomitant of the curve of distribution—for if children vary from an average, there must be some below that average as well as others above it—it takes its place in the scheme of things. Far from being an abnormality, it is only to be expected that each class should contain some backward children, and this knowledge can be very helpful to young teachers in removing fear and guilt. Once they are

[1] Similar caution is necessary if training college students attend a Child Guidance Clinic and help with play groups: what they are doing is not play therapy and should not be so called.

re-assured that it is not a shortcoming in them that the backward children are as they are, and that nobody expects them to achieve a comparable standard from all the children, they are more likely to feel free enough to wish to help such children without defensiveness and without over-anxiety. To *wish* to help—that is the first stage on the road that leads to providing effective support, and although it may be some time before the student is skilled enough to do this, yet without the wish there would be no incentive to learn, but rather repression and denial as in the case of Head Teacher F in an earlier chapter. I have been struck by the frequency with which teachers at all levels seek to deny that any of their pupils can fail (unless indeed they are pupils whom they have rejected), no doubt because that failure is subconsciously conceived as striking a blow at their own competence. Perhaps in the last analysis the root cause of the unpopularity of teaching backward children is that it can undermine the teacher's confidence in himself and the efficacy of his methods unless he is either quite insensitive or unusually firmly grounded in his integrity. Possibly that is one reason why teachers of backward children tend to be either very bad or very good—the average ones are more likely to choose to work with children whose achievements can buttress their self-respect. It takes a good teacher to accept the challenge to his skill which backward children present, but at the same time a poor teacher who works with them is tempted to use their backwardness as an excuse for his own low standards.

I do not wish to suggest that all that is required to remove this repression of failure is knowledge of the normal curve of distribution! since obviously the root causes lie elsewhere. But at least one can hope that sensible factual knowledge of this kind can be helpful to a student in forming his basic attitudes, particularly if it is linked with a general philosophy of education which stresses the importance of each individual, even if he is handicapped ('are not two sparrows sold for a farthing?') One should add that he is more likely to incorporate such ideas into his own attitudes if he sees that those who teach him are not themselves unduly defensive about rather weak students. It may seem rather far-fetched to suggest that those who are responsible for the guidance of students may do more in the long run to help them accept the necessity for individual variation if they are themselves prepared to expect and allow for individual variation, than by the most detailed discussion of the causes of backwardness, but I believe it to be true. Elaborate discussions of the causes of backwardness at the training college stage are all right as far as they go, but (1) they are often rather unreal problems to the student, (2) they may cause revulsion rather than interest, or a morbid interest, (3) they leave his root attitudes untouched. More genuine and lasting interest comes, if it comes at all, with greater maturity, and real experience of the conditions. I believe a safer way in the training colleges is to stress that individual differences imply differing educational expectations, without going into detailed specifications.

A point of view rather different from the one adopted here has been set out by Mr L. W. Downes in a symposium on teacher training in *The Bulletin of Education* (May 1953) to which he and I contributed.[1] He advocates a course in the teaching of backward children as part of the initial training of students, and describes one with which he is associated and which in the year of which he wrote was taken by a sizeable proportion (40 per cent) of his second year men. With much of what he says regarding the necessity of extending the scope of the education course so that it includes instruction in reading method I entirely agree, but it then seems to me that he reaches

---

[1] I am grateful to Mr Downes and to the Editor of the *Bulletin* (now renamed *Education for Teaching*) for permission to use material from this symposium.

wrong conclusions because he confuses the initial teaching of reading with backwardness in reading. It is highly desirable that men's colleges should encourage their students to learn how to help children to read, as a normal basic skill; but a detailed study of backwardness in reading is much more questionable.

Secondly, when from the mechanics of reading he moves on to the general content of his Backwardness course, some of his inclusions could be criticised as being too detailed and too specialised for the majority of beginner teachers. A student who has no standards of comparison to guide him is as unready to venture into this field as a dull five-year-old is to start formal reading. We condemn a student who gives unsuitable materials to the children: but it is important for all of us concerned in the training of teachers to make sure that we are not open to the same criticism at a different level, if we attempt to cram students with detailed specialities for which they are not yet ready. It is tempting to pack yet more and more into the education course arguing 'they will need to know this at some future time', but it is the *present* stage of development alone which is accessible to the educator. He builds for the future by giving only what the learner (child or student) is ready for and can assimilate *now*. Maturation and experience will deepen the learner's understanding, and then he can go further, but only if there is a solid foundation of assimilated material on which to build. I would myself prefer the much slower, but probably safer method, of using the initial training period to gain a good grasp of normal child development and of the wide variability which is consonant with normality, and treat backwardness only incidentally. It is much less striking, but there is less risk of superficial learning and hasty generalisation, and students losing their way in too much complexity of detail.

Thirdly, Mr Downes argues that since students are in fact, however undesirably, often given C classes when they leave college, it is well to recognise that fact and prepare them for it. This argument sounds more reasonable than it is, because if the practice is not defensible, it is foolish to connive at its continuance—rather what is wanted is a firm stand against it, above all from the training colleges.

Let us see how it works out in practice. Miss Evans is twenty and has just got her teaching certificate and this is her first post. The backward class she is given would try to the full the skill and patience of a more experienced teacher. Miss Evans has neither the personal maturity, the confidence in class management, the teaching skill nor the command of technique required. She does her best, but at the end of a year she thankfully relinquishes her class, which is taken over by the latest recruit, who will be disillusioned in his turn. That class remains a searing memory to Miss Evans and she has no wish to repeat the experience. Three years later when she could have coped with it successfully, she is offered a backward class and refuses it. She has 'had it'—and incidentally so has the Headmaster, perhaps not undeservedly. I know that I could not have handled a backward class successfully at that stage myself and if we are honest that is probably true of most of us. This short-sighted policy of some Head Teachers is largely responsible for the unwillingness of experienced teachers to take backward classes, for it becomes part of their pattern of accepted beliefs that prestige and experience are associated with 'promotion' to a brighter class. So a vicious circle is set up, as the children become more and more troublesome under inexperienced handling and as the years pass with their genuine difficulties of learning unresolved, and as the younger teachers assimilate the rejection of those who can't succeed which they see among their elders.

A clear lead from the Local Authorities to bring this practice to an end is what is wanted, not half-hearted compromises with it. After all, the Local Authorities have power to supervise and guide probationer teachers as well as to control the staffing of schools, and it is difficult to believe that these powers are taken seriously if glaringly bad placements by individual Heads continue unchecked. But although the major responsibility rests with the Authorities, those concerned with the training of teachers can do much by loud and repeated protests to raise informed opinion against the practice. To set up a course on backwardness to meet a need which should not be encouraged to continue seems short-sighted.

I have suggested that the present system of 'the weakest to the wall' ends in the perpetuation of undesirable attitudes to backwardness, among many teachers in many schools, and it would seem preferable policy for training colleges to concentrate on three objectives. Starting with the most easily attainable, and gradually widening, they are as follows: (1) Students should be given adequate grounding in methods of teaching the basic subjects. (2) Great importance should be attached to the formation of an attitude of sympathetic acceptance of individual differences. This lies at the root of all desirable attitudes to backwardness, and in the last resort is the only way in which the undesirable attitudes can be routed. (3) A campaign to educate public opinion in the schools and education offices against the undesirability of handing the most difficult classes to the least experienced teachers.

In-Service Training. It is both easier and harder to discuss questions of backwardness with a group of experienced teachers than it is with young students—easier because there is more knowledge based on experience, harder because the acquired attitudes of the teacher have often hardened. The first point is obvious, but the second is not always given as much recognition as it deserves, yet the teacher's attitude is basic to any real consideration, particularly where re-education is concerned. I have suggested that the climate of opinion in many schools is unfavourable to the development of a sympathetic attitude to backward children, partly for reasons of traditional prestige, but not wholly on that account—below the 'social' unpopularity of the backward class, it is probable that there is a deeper sub-stratum of rejection which is rooted in the individual teacher's need to be reassured that he is valuable and competent. So the psychological component, the basic insecurity, reinforces the social value system and provides much of its resistance to change. It would be theoretically possible to map out the various influences which have been at work in determining the full-grown attitude of each teacher— his early upbringing, his own successes and failures, and whether these led to defensiveness or sympathy; what was taught him in his training course; what was taught him less formally but perhaps more surely, by the collective judgments of the other teachers in the various schools in which he worked—but such an undertaking would hardly commend itself as being practicable to a Local Authority which wanted to provide a short evening course on backwardness for its teachers. To go to the other extreme, it would be quite practicable for an Authority to arrange such a course, concentrating *entirely* on a discussion of techniques and leaving out of account the attitudes of the teachers attending. It would be quite practicable (and is indeed common), but is it useful? A workable compromise would appear to be that the discussion of techniques should indeed occur, but in a context which related them to the attitudes and needs of both teachers and children; and that those responsible for conducting the course should bear in mind that the best methods will fail, not only if they do not appeal to the children, but also if they do not appeal to the teachers. In other words, what is needed is not *only* the dissemination of information regarding useful ways of helping backward children, desirable and necessary though that is; to be fully effective it is important that the teachers' attitudes should be favourable, for knowledge of the *means* of helping is more likely to be utilised by those who *want* to help backward children.

What I am suggesting is that *direct* attacks by the provision of courses on an unpopular problem like backwardness will have only a limited success unless they are accompanied by indirect measures on the part of the Authority to overcome that unpopularity, for example:

1. Giving the young teacher a fair deal in his first appointment. This has already been discussed, and will not be repeated here, except to say that I believe it to be one of the most important causes of bad attitudes later. If that could be cut away at the root, the battle against the unpopularity of backwardness might well be half won.

2. Stressing the social importance of the task. As long as people think only in terms of teaching the three R's at an abnormally slow pace, it is not surprising that it sounds very dull! But if it is thought of in its context as a form of social service, as salvaging a child who needs special help to overcome his handicaps both inherent and environmental, it is as meritorious as, and much more difficult than, helping a normal child to develop his powers. This would, however, imply that the goals of schools should be wider than just scholastic results, and this in its turn implies that Authorities should set the tone in this respect.

3. Increasing the prestige of those who teach backward children. It is hoped that one of the effects of instituting long courses for experienced senior teachers leading to University Diplomas in the teaching of subnormal and other handicapped children will be to increase the regard in which teachers of backward children are held. But such courses are few and of their nature can be attended by only a limited number of teachers, though by acting as a leaven, it is hoped that these teachers can exert an influence out of proportion to their numbers. Another method of increasing prestige is to stress

that posts in special education are given to teachers of high professional standing. For instance, a small Authority with one special E.S.N. school has over a number of years insisted that only successful teachers shall be considered for appointment there, and in consequence it is considered an honour to be selected to teach educationally subnormal children. This is excellent if it can be done, but it is not always feasible, particularly if an Authority has a large number of posts to fill and the market is poor. Turning from special schools to ordinary schools, the position becomes even more difficult. One expedient is to emphasise the 'special-ness' of certain posts, for example in transfer classes. This has been successful up to a point, and I think it is fair to say that such classes are now usually well regarded, but the trouble is that there is not much carry-over from them to the D streams, and it is these which form the hard core of the problem of prestige.

4. Similar remarks apply to the question of providing good working conditions. It is one thing to see that conditions are attractive in a few special cases, but quite another to ensure that all who work with backward children have reasonably good facilities—but it is this latter which will be the touchstone of the final effectiveness of the Authority's policy.

It would be over-optimistic to hope that these measures can be put into effect immediately, or that if they were, they would result in a sudden improvement in the general climate of opinion among teachers. Attitudes that have been built up over the years change slowly, and we are suffering from decades of considering scholastic results only, and of thinking that backward children can be taught by the youngest teachers, or by those who, though older, are unsuccessful, using whatever equipment and books are left over when the other classes have had their pick. Nevertheless, it is only by reversing them in the policy of Authorities, that the effects in improved attitudes will gradually be felt. On this as a basis, plans can be made for in-service training. This is much easier to talk about, as it is more direct and of obvious utility, but the imponderables which we have been discussing are a prerequisite for any real attack on the problem. They may have sounded vague, but I believe them to be important.

We turn now to the content of short evening courses on backwardness for serving teachers, such as might be arranged by a Local Authority, or by the extra-mural department of a University and attended by teachers whose interest in backward children may be very deep, or may be rather slight. At this stage a number of topics, which could not well be included in the initial training course on account of the inexperience of the students, can appropriately be discussed—details of organisation and management in a class which contains a wide range of ability and attainment, the relation between backwardness and delinquency and other forms of social failure, problems of motivating slow and dull children, methods of assessment and diagnosis (including particularly how to deal with the problems after they have been diagnosed), legal and social aspects, co-operation with other persons outside the school whose services it may be useful to know of and to call on, and so on. On each of these topics the teachers attending will be able to offer opinions based on their experience, and the main function of the course is to systematise and refine those opinions by linking them with what may be regarded as known facts—legislation, psychological data, the results of previous educational experiments, the advantages and drawbacks of various teaching methods, and so forth. It is important that the treatment of all topics should be practical and attuned to classroom conditions, and not deal merely in general statements, or in enunciating ideals which are unlikely to be realised: similarly, details of testing techniques should not be overweighted. Discussion of individual children can be utilised to serve two valuable functions: on the one hand it drives home in the most convincing of all ways the fact of individual differences, and the complexity of the issues involved in each case, so that snap generalisations are not possible. At the same time, it helps the teacher to identify himself with the particular child whose circumstances he is setting out, so that he presents the material from the child's point of view and almost insensibly comes to ask himself 'How would *I* like it if this happened to me?' and this can be valuable in enlarging his sympathies, particularly if, as often happens, he chooses a child whom he was inclined to reject on account of unacceptable habits or behaviour. To see things from the child's point of view—in a sense it may be said that this is the goal of the course, for even if the course is too short for much factual information and knowledge to be purveyed, it has achieved a great deal if this is one of its results. A change of focus, an accession of interest, an increased readiness to see backward children as individuals—these work from within outwards, and are perhaps more likely to carry over into the teacher's dealings with his class than a mass of external information. This is not to say that information is not of value, but it is best to keep it fairly straightforward and to avoid superior-sounding polysyllables such as 'constitutional inferior', 'a bad case of alexia', 'congenital auditory imperception', 'hereditary taint', and the like. These are superficially impressive, but they don't really help us to deal with Tommy, and what is worse, they increase our emotional distance from him. At the same time, information regarding methods and techniques of teaching is needed, but here again emphasis should be placed on the simplest expedients first. As was suggested in the previous chapter, there is a danger at the present time of teachers becoming too tentative in their approach to children who are basically normal, though backward, because they have 'heard of' so many alarming complications that they are almost afraid to teach them. A short course should be reassuring to the teachers who attend it in the sense that it limits the number of possibilities raised to those which they are most likely to meet and be able to deal with, at the same time making it clear that there are exceptional difficulties which require exceptional measures that are beyond their competence, and that the sensible thing in such cases is to refer the matter promptly to the appropriate Authority. This seems to be a wiser plan than to attempt to cover in an inevitably superficial manner, a large number of unlikely eventualities, for the plain fact is that if the teachers are confused and unsure what they can do safely, they are very likely to end by doing nothing. It is most important to build up the teachers' confidence in the children, and in their own ability to handle them successfully, for insecure teachers are unlikely to be able to give effective help. (In passing, it has been said that just as parents have been made insecure by vague talk of untold damage to their offspring, so teachers are similarly being affected. There may very well be something in this.) Whatever else can or cannot properly be expected at the end of a short course, at least those who have attended should feel more and not less confident of their ability to meet the children's need. Confidence, of course, is not the same thing as cocksureness, which is never appropriate, however lengthy the training.

Finally, more specialised training is necessary for those who seriously desire to make work with subnormal children their career. The Report of the National Advisory Council on the Training of Teachers[1] makes this clear, and recommends appropriate measures as to courses, qualifications, and so forth. To meet the need, full-time courses have been set up at a number of Universities and others are planned. It is easiest to write of what one knows personally, and so I will give a short account of the content and aims of the London course, which

[1] *The Training and Supply of Teachers of Handicapped Pupils*, November 1954.

was started in 1950 at the request of the Local Education Authorities within the Area Training Organisation, who were perturbed by the problems presented by backwardness within their special and ordinary schools.

The teachers who come to the course are persons of some standing and seniority. They are not accepted with less than five years' experience and in fact most of them have had much more than this minimum, preferably with normal as well as with subnormal children and with different age-groups. About half are teaching in E.S.N. schools and the remainder come from other types of special schools where backwardness is a problem and from infant, junior and secondary modern schools. They are seconded by their Authority on full salary: this means that mature men and women with family responsibilities are enabled to come, and it also means that Local Authorities, faced with a considerable outlay for each selected teacher, for the most part select very carefully those whom they recommend for admission.[1]

Considerations of selection seem to me of fundamental importance in this kind of course. As it was the first one-year course at University level to be started in England, and as it leads to a University Diploma, there are many more applicants than there are places. Since it could never conceivably cover *every* teacher in E.S.N. schools, and still less those who are dealing with educationally subnormal children in ordinary schools, we feel that the most beneficial way of using the places on the course is to select those who are capable themselves in their turn of acting as leaders. We try to choose teachers who will not only do good work themselves on their return to the schools, but who will be able to help other teachers in their district and who are sufficiently senior for their opinions and

[1] The really hard-hit candidates are the ones who are living away from home while on the course, and who have to maintain two establishments.

practices to carry weight. The average age is in the later thirties, but ranges up to fifty, and very few come younger than thirty. On the whole, the older ones are the most successful, for a younger teacher, however 'bright', cannot compete with a *good* older person in depth and variety of experience. They show much greater resilience and willingness to learn than one might have expected from a mature group, and some of them have been of high calibre, both as regards character and performance. There has been evident among them what I can best describe as informed idealism—practical, steady, and emotionally adult as distinct from merely vague and well-meaning—and indeed, those who deliberately and of set choice take up and remain in work which most teachers regard as unattractive are likely to have well-tried convictions. For what it is worth, my impression on following them up is that most of them continue to develop not only while they are at the Institute of Education, but also after they have returned to their schools.

In planning the content of the course, an effort was made to combine theoretical study at University level with a close and continuing linkage with the schools, so that a teacher's reading is never divorced from a practical context. During the first two terms, theory and practice go forward together, and the third term consists of eight weeks of continuous teaching, followed by a concluding period back at the Institute, and ending in the Diploma examination. For convenience, the various topics will be described in the following order—practical work (visits: sessional work in schools: surveys: continuous teaching) and theoretical studies, as long as it is realised that these are not carried on separately but side by side (except for block teaching).

1. Visits to schools and other social institutions and ancillary services take place once a week for the first two terms. It is worth stressing that visiting is one of the most potent means

by which experienced teachers learn. They have the background of knowledge to make use of visits in a way which is impossible for a beginning student, and whereas teachers normally spend all their time shut up between four walls of one building, a training course enables them to compare and contrast, and form standards of criticism and judgment by which, when they return to their own school, they can see whether it stands up well or badly to the norm of those they have seen. But it would be a waste of opportunity if visits were confined only to schools, and schools of the type to which they are accustomed. So the programme begins with general visits designed to increase the teacher's knowledge of various facets of the educational system, for instance, schools and nurseries for young normal children (knowledge of whose methods can be so useful in teaching the educationally subnormal), various types of special schools (other than those for the educationally subnormal), clinics and social provisions for leisure, for vocational advice, for welfare. The second term's visits are entirely concerned with E.S.N. schools and classes, and the perspective of the first term's general visits is helpful in evaluating the work of the E.S.N. schools, and in bringing home to the teachers the interdependence of their work with that of other welfare services.

2. Another session each week is taken up with *practical work,* mainly in primary schools, in the assessment, diagnosis, and treatment of educational disabilities, with particular emphasis on remedial techniques in reading. Each teacher is attached to one school for the whole of the first two terms and works there with particularly backward children.

3. *Surveys.* Lectures on legal aspects of, for instance, exclusion of seriously difficult children are all very well, but they need to be supplemented by a knowledge of how things work in practice in one's own area, and so each teacher makes a simple survey of his own district. While the main emphasis

of such a survey is on educational provision in special schools and ordinary schools, many teachers widen the scope of their survey and include such topics as the provision of leisure activities for backward adolescents; facilities for the welfare and after-care of handicapped pupils; the extent and local handling of delinquency; mechanisms for vocational placement, etc. The value of the surveys is not simply that the teachers learn what services exist, but that they meet the *people* who administer them, with a consequent gain in understanding and readiness for co-operation.

4. *A continuous period of teaching* may on the face of it seem rather odd for teachers as experienced as these are. Surely, it will be said, they do not need 'school practice' which savours rather of the young raw beginner? But, in fact, it is a most valuable part of the course. During the eight weeks the teacher can put into practice the ideas which he has gained from his reading, by discussion with other teachers, through his study of remedial techniques, and from his visits, without the responsibility that a teacher in his own school is bound to feel limiting his freedom to experiment. It also affords an opportunity for him to widen his experience by teaching in a type of school that is new to him, for instance by taking a backward class in an approved school, or by a short period of residential work, without feeling that he is committed to remain there.

In considering the theoretical studies, it must be remembered that the training of mature persons differs from that of young students since greater emphasis will be placed on the testing of principles in the light of their own experience and less on the mechanical acquisition of theoretical knowledge. So, the teachers are required to think as well as read, and to assimilate matter which is meaningful to them through their previous knowledge, rather than to acquire isolated pieces of information. It is quite obvious that any course of training will concern itself with specialised techniques for teaching the basic subjects, but it is important that it should not stop there, but should place them within a wider context. The teachers must receive sufficient physical and psychological information for them to understand the causes of the child's disability and the treatment which it is receiving (where this is appropriate) and the effect of his handicap on him as a person. From a study of the child in his natural environment and habitat, the teachers learn always to think of schooling as a stage in the process of growth and not simply as a matter of curricula. Thus on the one hand, the teachers are gaining a wider viewpoint from which to regard their work, but at the same time they are kept down to earth by practical work with children, and by detailed study of remedial techniques, so that any tendency towards merely theoretical learning is counteracted.

We find that the teachers learn a great deal from each other, as the mere bringing together of a number of teachers from different areas, with experience of different ages of children under different Authorities and in different sorts of schools, is itself a most broadening influence. Set lectures tend to be replaced by discussions in which information can be pooled, and I think it is fair to say that teachers gain from the course in proportion to what they are prepared or able to contribute to it.

It must be remembered that this and other long courses start with the great advantage that their members are in no doubt about their desire to work with backward children, and it would be unwise to generalise too widely from them, but at least it can be said with confidence that older teachers who wish to learn can make excellent learners.

How effective any of this will turn out to be, it is impossible to say at present. One can be more optimistic with regard to the future of special E.S.N. schools which are (relatively) few in number and which are enviably untrammelled by considerations from which the ordinary schools can never (and should never) entirely free themselves, so that they can develop in their own way. But when one turns to the prospects of special educational treatment in the ordinary schools, one is liable to be assailed by doubts. The numbers are so great that the problem seems intractable. Of one thing I am convinced, and that is that the C and D classes and their teachers, particularly in the junior schools, hold the key to the future. If it can be shown that effective special educational treatment can be given under what one may call 'standard' conditions of numbers, equipment, etc. (in the sense that such conditions are reproducible in many other schools), then there is a chance. What happens under *better* conditions, however impressive, is a side issue, if those conditions are not reproducible on a large scale.

In the long run it is the quality of teaching, rather than the conditions, which will decide the outcome. Additional training may help those who do the most responsible work, in special schools, or as leaders and pathfinders in ordinary schools; but the majority who teach the lower streams in ordinary schools will be influenced by their training colleges, and by the efforts of their Local Authority to see that opinions and practices in the schools are favourable to the development of sympathetic attitudes to the less fortunate children. In the last analysis, special educational treatment depends not on policy and organisation, but on the human qualities of the teachers, and in a book concerned with policies, it is as well to end on this note.

Selected References

OFFICIAL SOURCES

Parliamentary

Education Act, 1944. H.M.S.O.

Mental Health Act, 1959. H.M.S.O.

Ministry of Education

Education in 1955, H.M.S.O. 1956.

School Health Services and Handicapped Pupils Regulations (Statutory Instrument No. 1156). H.M.S.O. 1953.

The Training and Supply of Teachers of Handicapped Pupils (Report of the National Advisory Council on the Training and Supply of Teachers). H.M.S.O. 1954.

Pamphlets:

No 5 *Special Educational Treatment*. H.M.S.O. 1946.
No 18 *Reading Ability*. H.M.S.O. 1950.
No 30 *Education of the Handicapped Pupil, 1945–55*. H.M.S.O. 1956.

The Health of the School Child (Report of the Chief Medical Officer of the Ministry of Education for the years 1952–53). Chapters 7 and 8. H.M.S.O. 1954.

BOOKS AND ARTICLES

BURT, C. *The Subnormal Mind*. 2nd edn. O.U.P. 1944.

CLEUGH, M. F. *Psychology in the Service of the School*. Methuen, 1951.

ed. CLEUGH, M. F. *Teaching the Slow Learner* (3 vols.). Methuen, 1961.

KIRK, S. AND JOHNSON, G. O. *Educating the Retarded Child*. Houghton Mifflin, 1951.

National Society for the Study of Education. 49th Yearbook, Part II. *The Education of Exceptional Children*. Univ. of Chicago Press, 1950.

PARKYN, G. W. *The Consolidation of Rural Schools*. N.Z. Council for Ed. Research, 1952.

WINTERBOURN, R. *Educating Backward Children in New Zealand*. N.Z. Council for Ed. Research, 1944.

Articles on Remedial Centres in:

1. *British Journal of Educational Psychology*, June 1950, November 1951, February 1953, November 1953.

2. *Educational Review of the Birmingham Institute of Education*, Vol. VI, Nos. 1, 2 and 3.

Symposium on Teacher Training in *Bulletin of Education*, May 1953.

Report on *The Social Adaptation of E.S.N. School Leavers* (National Association of Mental Health) (duplicated).

Index

aftercare, 81, 180
age of transfer, 15 ff.
arithmetic, 153, 165
ascertainment, chap. II, 61
attainments, 23 ff., 108, 109, 148 ff.
attitudes, 85 ff., 91, 93, 121, 166, 169 ff., 182

basic subjects, 42, 102, 114, 135, 147 ff., 170, 181
behaviour problems, 24 ff., 73 ff.
Birch, L. B., 140, 142
break at 11+, chap. IV, 98, 100, 162
Burt, C., 77
Butler, W. E. T., 43

certification, 57
Child Guidance Clinics, 127, 148, 153, 159, 165
Clarke, A. D. B. and A. M., 67
clubs, 82
Collins, J. E., 140
comprehensive schools, 157
confidence, 175, 176
continuity, importance of, 44, 144
cross-classification, 33
Curr, W., 140
Curtis Report, 50

de-ascertainment, 34, chap. V
defensiveness, 166, 167, 171
delinquency, 26, 48, 80, 174, 180
Downes, L. W., 167, 168

Education Act 1944, 2, 3, 6, 7, 51, 53, 59 ff., 92, 125
educational subnormality, connotation of, 6 ff., 51
escape clause, 74 ff.
exclusion, 19, 62, 73 ff.
extent of problem in ordinary schools, 89 ff., 113, 114, 118 ff.

Farrelly, E. D., 9

flexibility, 35, 96, 116, 126, 130, 155, 178

goals of endeavour, 48, 55, 63, 64, 172, 175
Gourlay, N., 140
guardianship, 80
Gulliford, R., 140

Hadow Report, 40
home conditions, 44, 61, 80

individual differences, 104 ff., 165, 170, 175
individual work, 32, 33, 96, 100, 148, 154
ineducability, 18, 67 ff.
'inexpedience', 62
insecurity, 49, 97, 99, 152, 166, 169, 171, 175-6
in-service training, 159, 170 ff.
institutional placement, 80
integration, 116, 134 ff., 158
intelligence tests, 18, 20 ff., 174

jurisdiction, 131, 145, 158

Kellmer, M. L., 140
Kemp, L. C. D., 103

leaving age, 64 ff.
Lendon, R. B., 9
liaison work, 143, 148 ff., 174

maladjustment, 25, 29, 54, 153, 159
Mental Deficiency Acts, 59 ff.
Mental Health Act, 61 ff., 78 ff.

National Association for Mental Health, 67
National Society for Mentally Handicapped Children, 67
non-readers, 133
normal development, 161, 165 ff.
normal distribution, 104 ff., 165, 166

opportunity classes, 85, 89, 124 ff.,
156
Orwin, C. S., 98

Parkyn, G. W., 98, 100
peripatetic advisers, 101, 157–8
practical work, 41, 45, 47, 114,
145
prevention of backwardness, 142,
159
principles, importance of, 4, 5

qualifications of teachers, 127,
128, 176 ff.
quality of provision, 89, 127, 128

reading, 42, 143, 154, 161 ff.
reading clinic, 148 ff.
records, 36, 39, 42, 149
remedial work, 52, 53, 56 ff., 91,
103, 114, 118, 123, 124, 132,
chap. X, 165, 179 ff.
reports to the Mental Health Committee, 16, 60, 62, 63, 66, chap.
VI, 179
repression, 166
residential schools, 17, 48 ff., 101
responsibility, 149 ff., 155
rural areas, 17, 48, 95 ff., 130

Schonell, F. J., 140, 164

segregation, 99, 132
selection procedures, 8 ff., 153, 177
sex ratio, 22, 31
simplicity, 39
social development, 97 ff., 116,
118, 144, 146
social services, 73, 172, 178, 179
special classes, 85, 86 ff., 92, 113,
114, chap. IX
specialisation, 116, 134 ff.
Stebbing, L. S., 72
stigma, 10, 26, 28, 57, 79, 117, 144
streaming, 32 ff., 92, 108 ff., 132 ff.
suitability, 90 ff., 119, 125
supervision, 61, 63, 79 ff.

Taylor, E. A., 4
teamwork, 132 ff.
Tizard, J., 67
Training Centres, 62, 68 ff.
Training Colleges, 160 ff.
transfer classes, 124 ff., 156, 173
transport, 46 ff., 126, 129, 149
trial period, 70

Valentine, H. B., 140
voluntary schools, 102, 103
voluntary supervision, 81

young teachers, 111, 127, 135
Youth Employment Service, 79